Human Versus Machine: Ho
Stockfish and Komoc

Part II

Copyright © 2017 Lyudmil Tsvetkov

All rights reserved. No part of this publication may be reproduced, stored in a retrieval system or transmitted in any form or by any means, electronic, electrostatic, magnetic tape, photocopying, recording or otherwise, without prior permission of the author.

Introduction

This is a collection of my winning games against Stockfish and Komodo. The games are played in the period 2013-2017 against different Stockfish versions and Komodo 10.

The games are for real. I have played over 50 thousand engine games, of which at least 10 thousand versus Stockfish, and a large number versus Komodo, so I have my fair share of wins.

Most of the games have been played on my 4-core computer. It is true that the hardware is nothing special, but rating lists affirm top engines are at least 3200 elos strong on such hardware, so one might suppose winning is quite a feat.

The time control for the games differs, but those are mostly blitz or rapid games, with myself having 2 times more on average on the clock. So, if Stockfish will have 3 minutes plus 2 seconds increment(all the games are played with increment) for the game, my time allocation will be 5 minutes plus 3 seconds, if Stockfish will have 5 minutes plus 3 seconds, my time allocation will be 10 minutes plus 5 seconds, etc.

There are no takebacks, and time control has been strictly applied.

If you follow the games carefully, you will be able to discover which openings are good for facing the top engines, how one should handle the game, what positional tricks to use and what tactical ones to avoid.

The games are amply commented and diagrammed. I suppose their quality is quite high, maybe even higher than World Championship level, but at the same time commentary puts a stress on only the most important lines and development of patterns, so I guess everyone having basic understanding of chess and some knowledge of tactics will be able to follow through them effortlessly.

Due to the nature of the task of having to beat overpowerful entities, I had to resort to contriving whole new systems of play, so you will only extremely rarely find similar positions in either human or engine games, if ever.

For most people, the verdict is made: 'Humans already don't stand a chance when facing top engines'. But this book shows otherwise. Maybe the contest is not finished yet, after all?

The second part features games against Stockfish DD, Stockfish 5, Stockfish 6 and Komodo 10.

To the 2 winning pawn structures, represented in the first part, King's Indian Defence/King's Indian Attack and Stonewall System/Stonewall Attack, another 2 are added, central closed structure, arising from Torre Attack(c3-d4-e5 central chain; the same could arise for black in the form of c6-d5-e4 central chain from the Slav), and English Opening closed structure(arising after both c4 and e4 have been played).

Openings vary, from Queen's Pawn Game and Reti, to Sicilian and Ruy Lopez, but most of them transpose to the abovementioned 4 structures.

I really think this book deserves careful investigation, as closed structures are the future of chess: they exhibit the deepest lines and most refined positional characteristics. That is one of the reasons top engines still have considerable difficulties with them.

Enjoy your time!

October 2017

Table of Contents

Introduction	2
Game 16 King foray	6
Game 17 Closed affair	25
Game 18 You are KIDding me	37
Game 19 No chance	57
Game 20 The powerful Torre	72
Game 21 The Berlin KID	87
Game 22 Dancing knights	100
Game 23 New paradigm	115
Game 24 I have a crush on you	134
Game 25 Too complicated	143
Game 26 Blunder Stockfish	162
Game 27 Fully blocked	173
Game 28 Astounding chain	192
Game 29 Positional squeeze	206
Game 30 Hitting the ball with the bat	221
Index of Games	238

Game 16
King foray

December 4th 2013
White: Lyudmil Tsvetkov
Black: Stockfish DD
D00 Queen's Pawn Game, transposing into Stonewall Attack

1. f4 Nf6 2. Nf3 d5 3. d4 e6 4. e3 c5 5. c3 Nc6 6. Bd3 Bd6 7. O-O O-O 8. Ne5

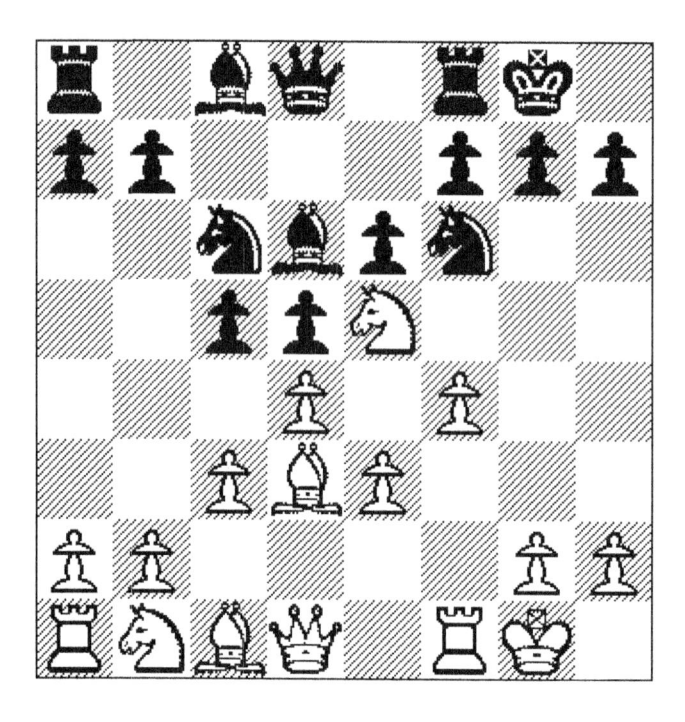

As already observed in Part I of this book, the Stonewall Attack is an excellent opening in trying to get a closed game against the silicon monsters, which, of course, only significantly boosts the human chances.

White has managed to place a mighty knight on the central e5 square, which is attacking the black king shelter and, what is even more important, seems uncapturable.

Qc7

This is a significant positional inaccuracy. Black should have played Ne4, to start struggling for the central squares. Now, white has the chance to prevent that jump, by taking sufficient control of the e4 point.

9. Nd2!

Of course, white ensures influence over e4. 9. Qf3 has also been possible.

b6 10. g4

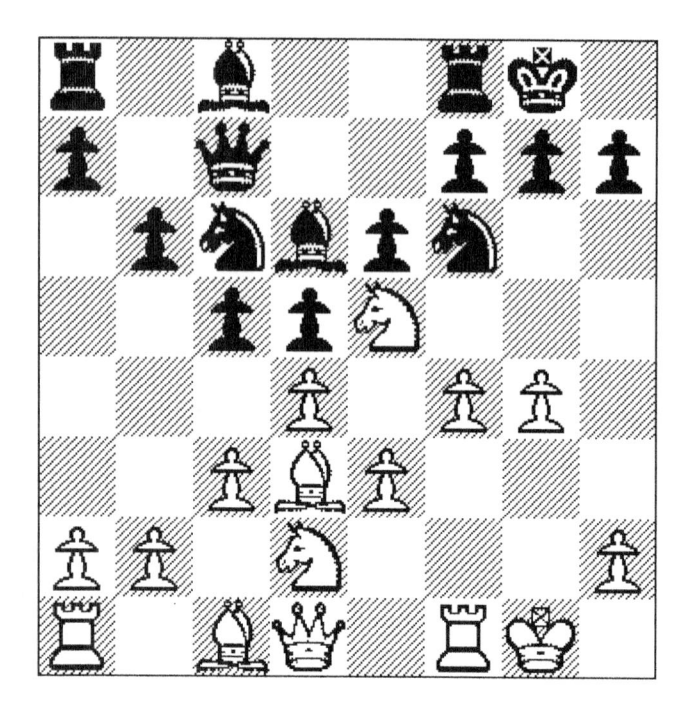

White starts an immediate attack, threatening g4-g5 with a tempo, and behold, the black knight can not go to e4, where is its natural place, so it must yield ground by retreating somewhere on a less advanced rank.

g6

To block the g5 storming pawn after g4-g5 is played, and possibly ensure possession of the h5 square for the knight.

11. g5 Nd7

11...Nh5 instead will pretty much lead to similar game development.

12. Rf3 Bb7

Completing development. Always develop before you do anything else.

13. Rh3

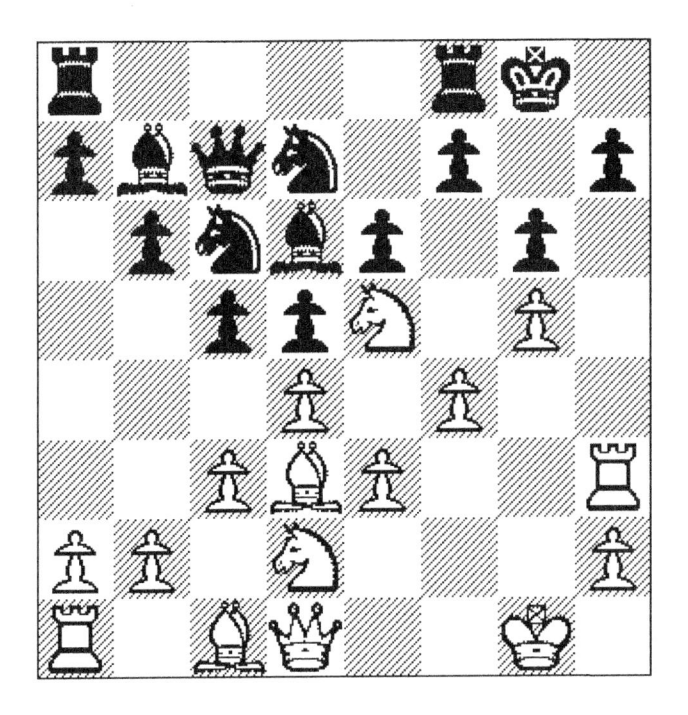

Stockfish has done that, but 3 white pieces, Ne5, Bd3 and Rh3, already directly attack the black king shelter. White is underdeveloped, but has sufficient positional advantages in return. That is how chess is played, trading one feature for another, nothing can ever be absolutised.

Be7

Taking the g5 pawn under control. 13...Ne7 14. Qg4 Nf5(attacking h4, so the queen can not go there) 15. Bf5 ef5 16. Qh4 h5 17. gh6, winning a pawn, might have been preferable, but white still retains quite some edge.

14. Qg4

White already has immediate threats(Rh6, followed by Qh4), so the opponent should do something to get rid of some of the numerous enemy attackers. Capturing the knight on e5 seems like a natural choice.

Nce5 15. fe5

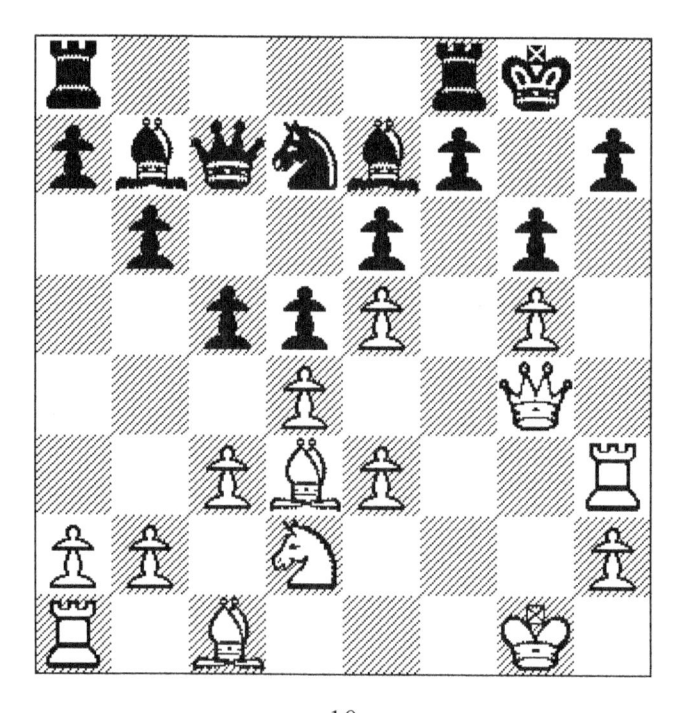

One advantage, having actively posted attacking pieces, has been transferred to another one: extremely weak f7 twice backward shelter pawn, making the shelter inflexible.

Qd8

The queen attacks the g5 pawn.

16. Nf3

Developing and defending g5.

Qc8

Stockfish aims at exchanging light-colour bishops after Ba6. 16...Kg7 17. Rh6(Qh6 h5) Rh8(to preemptively defend the h7 pawn) might have been somewhat better, but that would hardly alter the assessment of the position. Black is so pressed for space, especially on the king side, and under such a heavy attack, that saving the half point would be a miracle.

17. Rh6 Re8

Stockfish has another defensive plan in mind: to support h7 with the knight on f8, so the rook frees the f8 square.

18. Qh4 Nf8

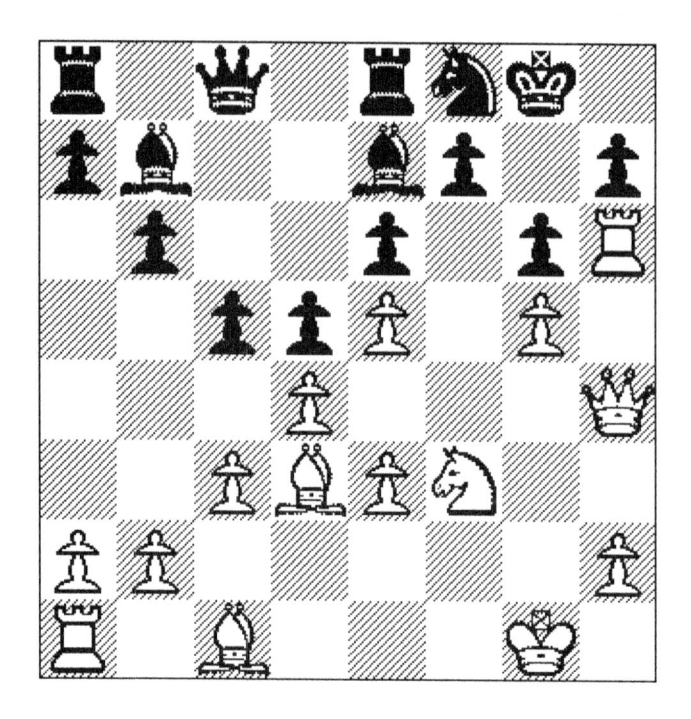

Well, the engine is extremely passive, but everything seems to be defended. White should bring additional forces into the assault.

19. Bd2 Ba6

Wanna change?

20. Bc2

Of course, the bishop retreats. Ba6 would not only leave white with a weak light-square complex, but also unnecessarily develop the black queen.

Be2!

The bishop not only attacks the knight on f3, but also clears the a6 square for the friendly queen to hop to.

21. Kf2!

The king gets active, right into the middlegame. It defends the f3 knight and clears the first line for the a1 rook. Although in the center, the white king is not exposed to any real danger, as the game is permanently closed.

Qa6

Preparing again trading of light-square bishops with Bd3.

21...Bf3 instead is an alternative(after all, black gets rid of one nasty white attacker, which, btw., could slow-jump at some point to f6 after h3, Nh2-g4), but that will hardly save black, as white retains the pair of bishops, and, after Qh4-g3, h2-h4-h5 will follow, gradually dismantling the passive black bastion.

22. Rg1

The queenside rook joins into the attack. Rg3-h3 threatens.

Bc4

A mysterious engine move, but there are not much better options.

22...Bd3 seemed like the natural choice, but then 23. Bd3(Bd1? Bf5, and the black bishop controls the h3 square, which will be inaccessible to the white rook) Qd3 24. Rg3 Qe4(offering exchange of queens) 25. Qh3, followed by Rg4 and Rh4/f4, depending on circumstances, should win for white.

23. Rg3

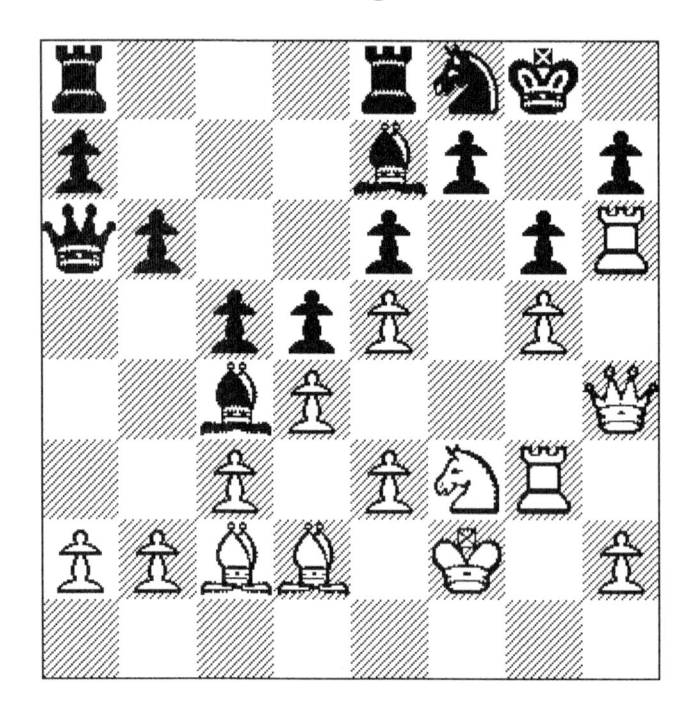

How does black prevent now Rg3-h3, followed by Rh7, with a rout?

Bf1!

Well, by lifting to the 3rd rank(Rg1-g3), the white rook has left the f1 square unattended, so the opponent bishop immediately makes use of that. Now, the h3 square is again under control.

Similar unobvious surprising moves are a trademark of engines and often missed by humans.

24. Rg1!

24...Qe2 check has been threatening, sending the white king to the 1st rank, so the king decides to bravely join the attacking forces via g3.

Qe2 25. Kg3

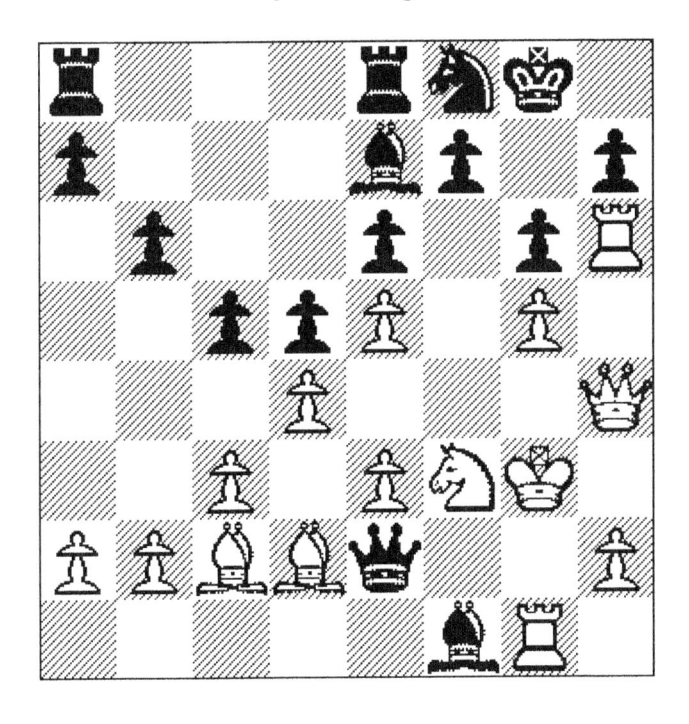

All white pieces are defended, so the queen-bishop penetration is not at all dangerous for it.

Rec8

Trying to create some counterplay on the half-open c file after cd4 ed4.

26. h3

Evacuating the h2 square, so the knight can jump to g4 via h2. Of course, this is currently impossible.

Bd8 27. Kf4

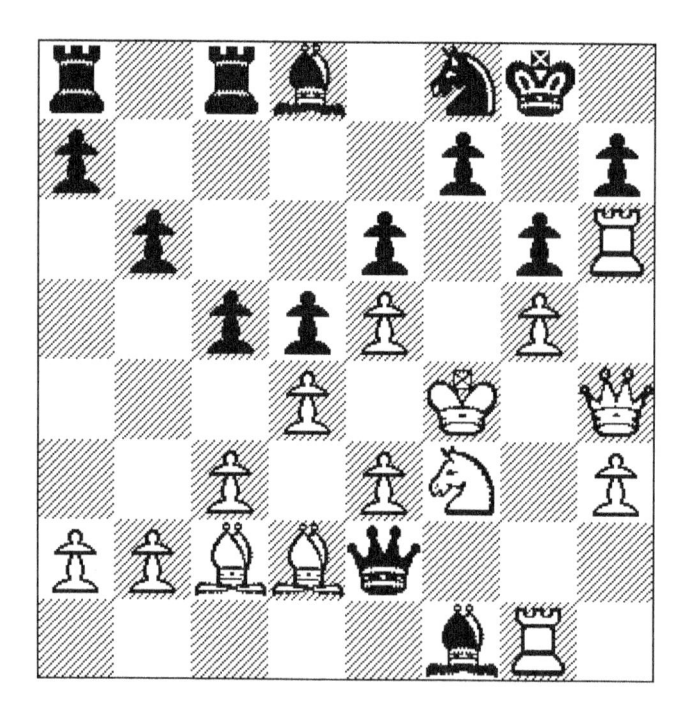

Funny position, is not it? I have not seen many like that. The king feels completely safe in the very heat of the battle. Kf4 has simultaneously cleared the h4-e1 diagonal, so white has the option of trading queens after Qe1 Qe1 Be1, with a winning endgame. This would have been the better choice for black, though.

Qa6?

Attacking the a2 pawn and aiming at Bd3, but that is very insufficient.

28. Qf2

The bishop on f1 is under double attack and should retreat.

Bc4 29. Nh2

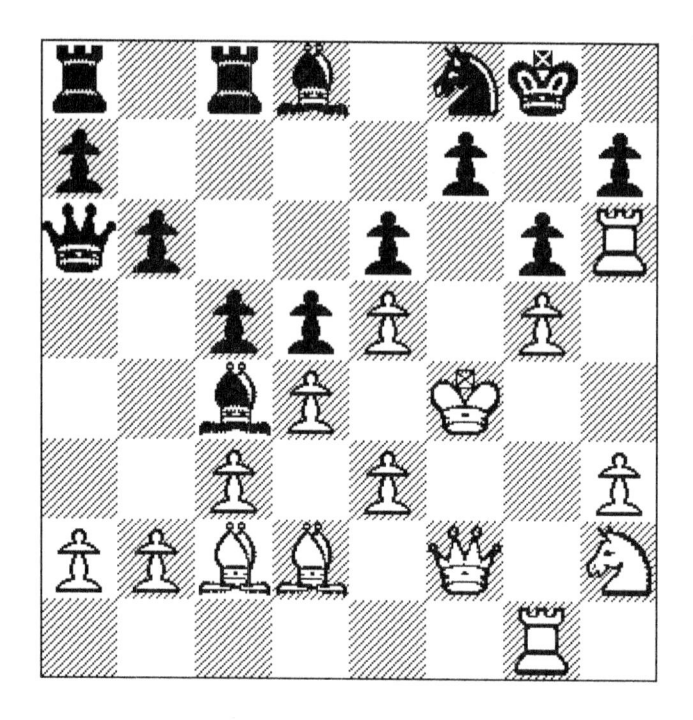

The knight takes its final route to f6.

Bd3

What else?

29...Qa2 30. Bc1 cd4 31. ed4 Bb3 32. Bb3 Qb3 33. Ng4, followed by Nf6 and Qh4 at some propicious tactical point or Rg4-h4, and white wins. Black gets mated either on h7, g7 or h8, for example 33...b5(seeking some counterplay) 34. Nf6 Bf6(Kg7/h8 Qh4) 35. gf6 b4 36. Qh4 bc3 37. Rh7! Nh7 38. Qh6, and black gets mated on g7.

30. Bd1

Bd3 is a major mistake, as after Qd3, the black queen penetrates on the light squares, threatening different extremely unpleasant checks.

Qa2

30...Bf5(Be4 is even worse, as has no purpose) 31. Be2(important prophylactic move, otherwise the black queen could have penetrated to d3) Qa2 32. Ng4, followed by Nf6 and Qh4 decides the game in the already mentioned way.

If 32...Bg4, then 33. hg4, opening the h file, with subsequent tripling of white heavies on it, and mate.

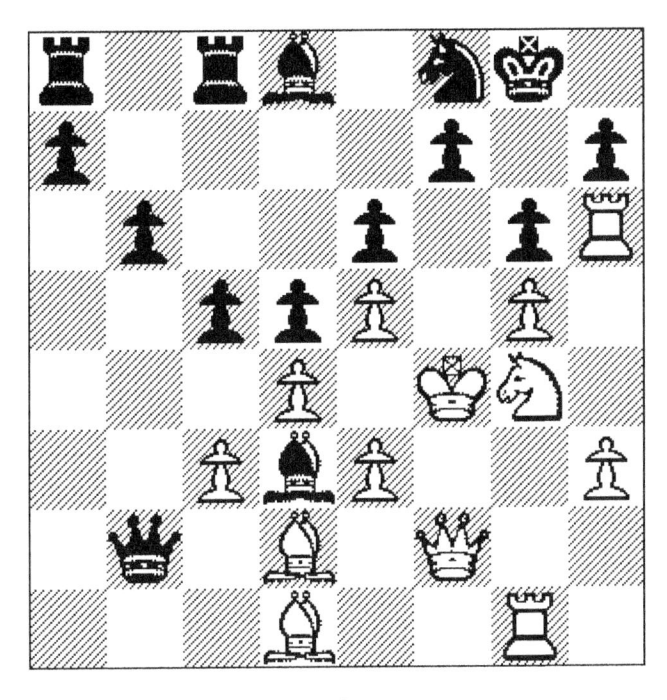

31. Ng4 Qb2

Black is too slow in its counterplay.

When one side has such a decisive positional advantage, winning lines are available one way or another, though concrete tactics are always to be searched for.

32. Nf6 Bf6 33. ef6

Much cleaner than gf6 g5! check Rg5 Ng6 countercheck, and suddenly things get too complicated. When playing a top engine, never think you have won the game, the engine might surprise you even at the very last moment, just deliver mate.

a5

A powerful thrust to promote the a passer. Stockfish likes playing with many queens.

33...e5 was an option, but will more or less lead to developments as in the game.

33...cd4! was seemingly the best try, opening the game and inviting unimaginable tactics, and I would hate to go through all lines after 34. cd4(ed4 Rc3! is much weaker, as white can not capture on c3 due to the queen on f2 hanging) Rc3!, or 34...e5 35. Ke5!(de5 Ne6 check Kf3 Qe5 is much weaker).

White should retain some advantage both in the middlegame due to abundant tactics, and in the endgame, due to its very active king, but the exact overlong lines are very difficult to figure out by a human.

34. Rg2

Defending the bishop on d2, so the queen can go to h4 to deliver mate.

a4

Stockfish continues with its wrong plan: obviously, it simply does not see mate.

35. Qh4 Kh8

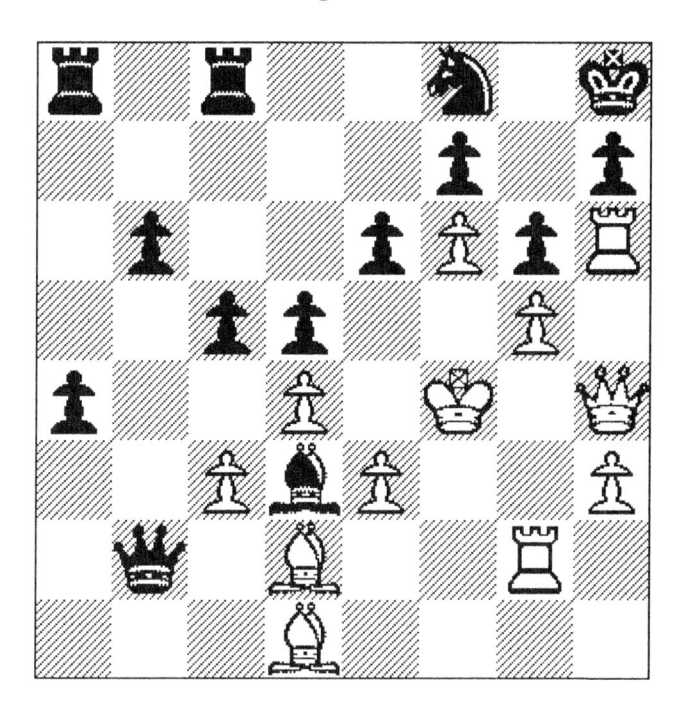

White has been threatening 36. Rh7 Nh7 37. Qh6, with mate on g7 to follow. Now, after Rh7 Nh7 Qh6, black has Rg8, protecting the g7 square.

A typical engine move, that seemingly defends everything, even in the most precarious of situations, but Stockfish has not seen far enough.

36. Rh7

Still.

Nh7 37. Qh6

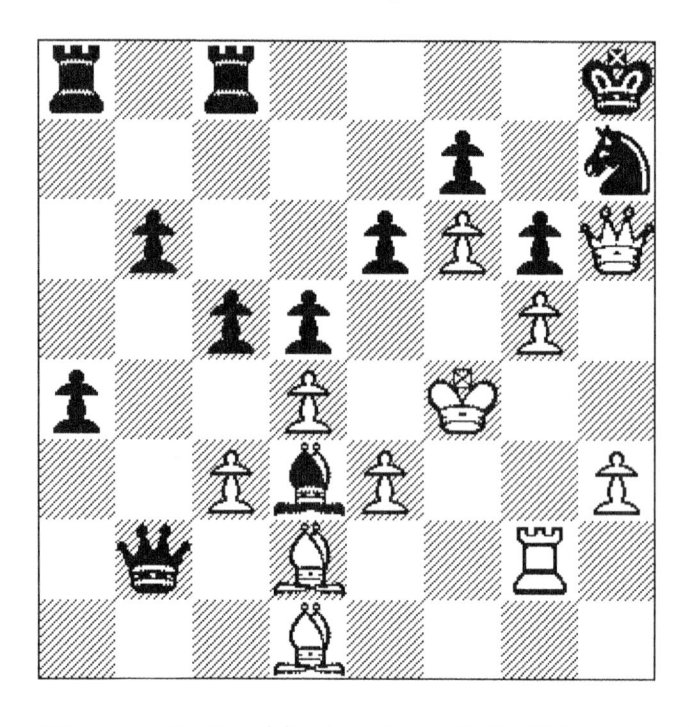

Now, on Rg8, white has Rg4! Qd2 Qh7! check Kh7 Rh4 mate(the black rook is blocking the g8 escape square).

e5

All black has is a couple of spite checks and interpositions.

38. de5 Rg8 39. Rg4 Be2 40. Be2 Qb4

Funny, is not it?

41. cb4 a3 42. Qh7 Kh7 43. Rh4 mate

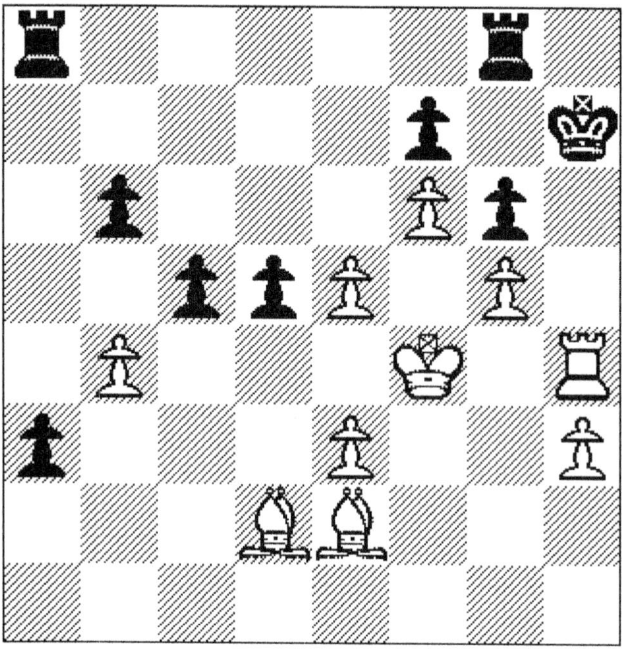

Game 17
Closed affair

December 4th 2013
White: Lyudmil Tsvetkov
Black: Stockfish DD
D00 Queen's Pawn Game

1. f4 Nf6 2. Nf3 d5 3. d4 e6 4. e3 c5 5. c3 Be7
6. Bd3 O-O 7. O-O c4 8. Bc2 b5 9. a3 Bb7
10. Ne5 Nc6 11. Nd2

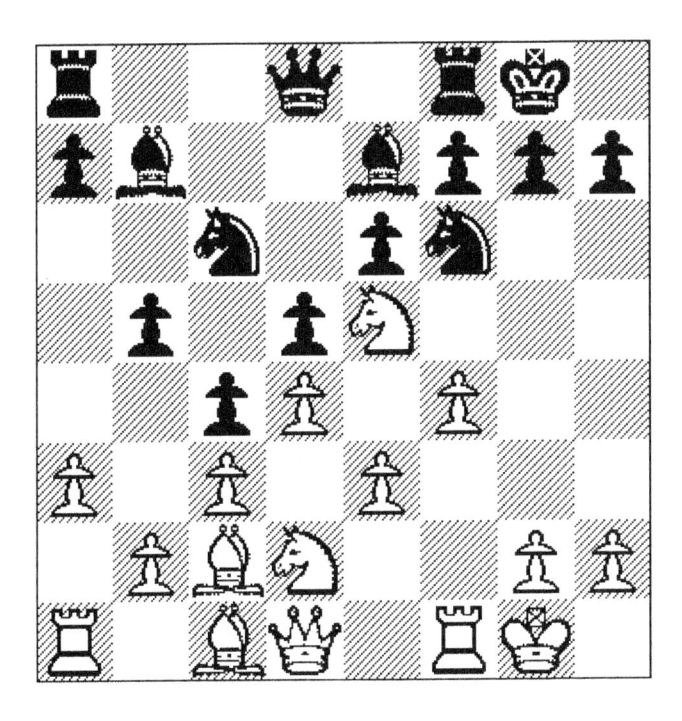

In a familiar setup, Stockfish has chosen again to close the game on the queen side.

25

Kh8

A strange move, to say the least.

Certainly, there were more promising choices, for example g6.

12. Qf3 Rc8 13. g4 a5 14. Rf2

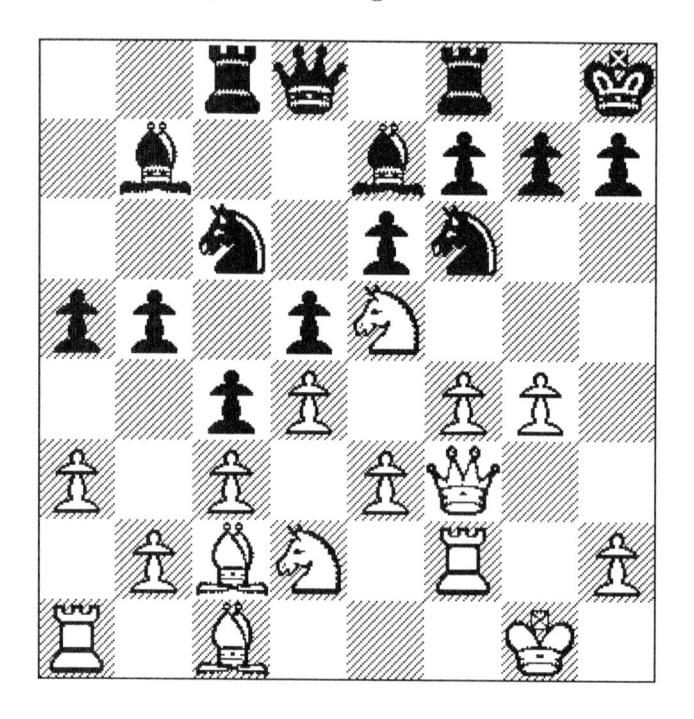

The rook heads to g2.

b4

Stockfish is active.

15. Rg2 b3

The engine gains as much space as possible, but it might have been wiser not to fully block the queen side.

16. Bb1

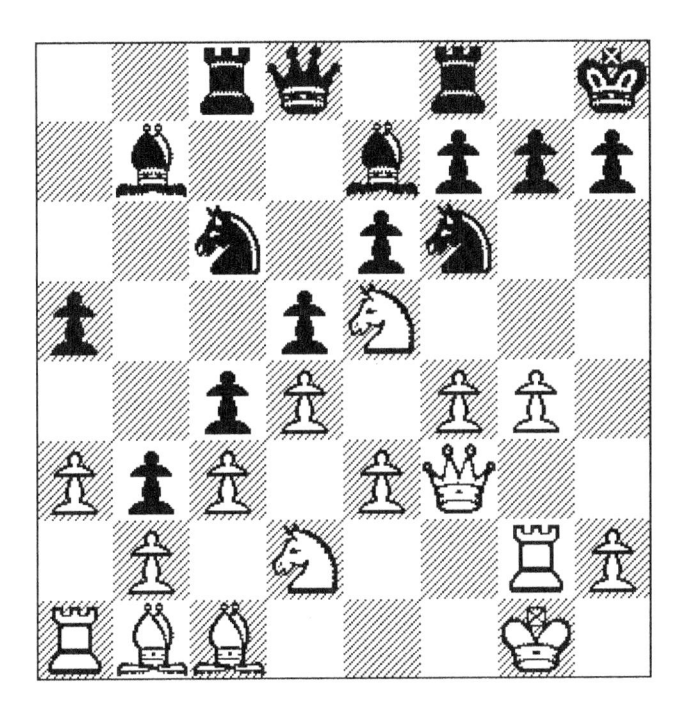

16. Bd1 might have been better, as now the rook on a1 is permanently trapped(for the reason that the bishop on b1 has no reasonable moves).

g6 17. g5 Ne5 18. fe5 Nh5 19. h4

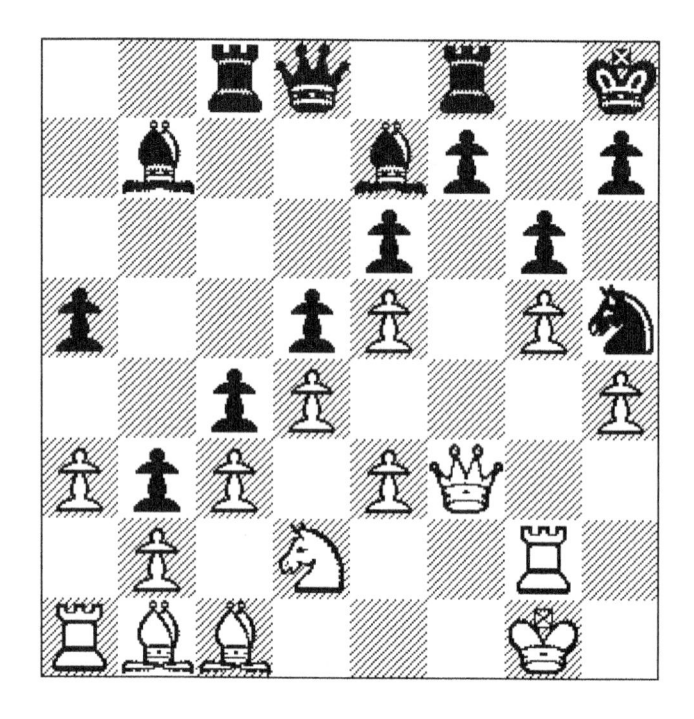

The setup is certainly familiar, though even more closed than usual.

That will test both sides' manoeuvering technique.

Rc7 20. Qg4 Ng7 21. Nf3 Qa8

Not the very best of manoeuvres, the queen has nothing to do on a8, but that is equally true for other board locations.

22. Rh2 Nh5

h4-h5 has been imminent.
The knight blocks the enemy pawn.

23. Rg2

To free the h2 square for the knight, from where it can go to g4 and f6.

**Bd8 24. Bd2 Rd7 25. Nh2 Bc6
26. Qf3 Rg8 27. Ng4**

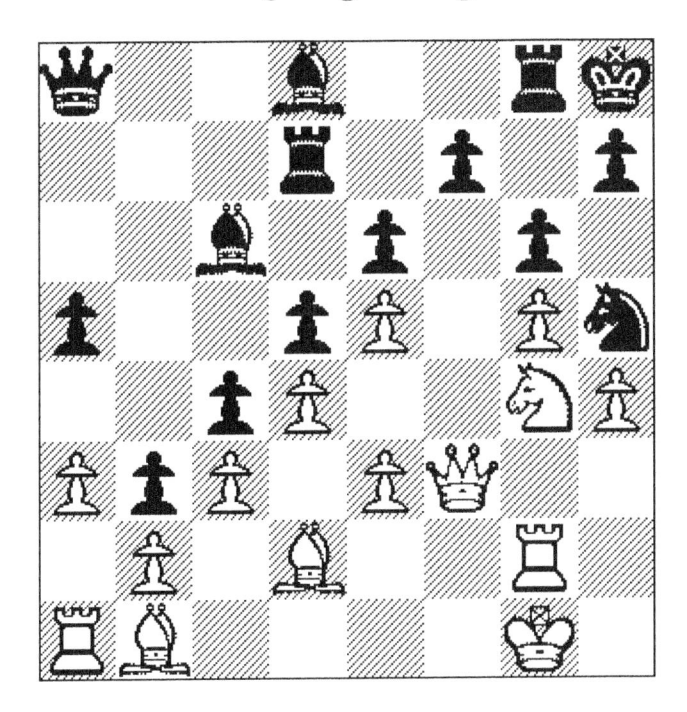

Indeed, the knight has jumped to g4.

The white advantage is evident, but how does it convert, provided that the bishop on b1 and the rook on a1 are more or less out of the game?

Bb6 28. Nf6 Nf6

28...Ng7 29. h5

29. gf6 Qf8 30. Qf4

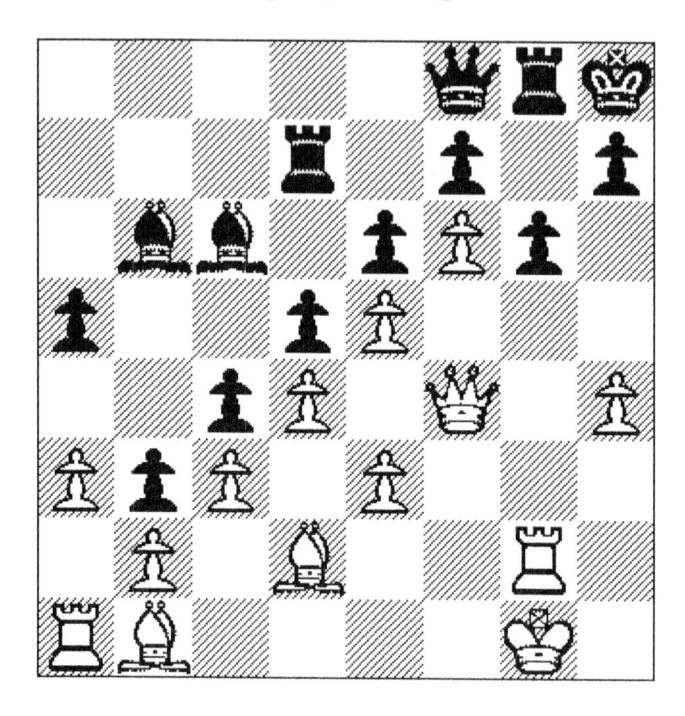

Another funny position.

Black has much more space, but that space is on the section of the board, where the kings are not, so useless.

It is difficult for Stockfish to recognise such subtle patterns.

Qd8 31. Kf2

Clearing the first rank.

The king is extremely safe in the center too.

Rc7 32. Rg5 Qf8 33. Rg2

White can shuffle for as long as it deems necessary.

Qd8 34. Kf1

This is not a shuffling move.
The king leaves the e1-h4 diagonal, for the dark-square bishop to transfer upon.

Qf8 35. Be1 h5

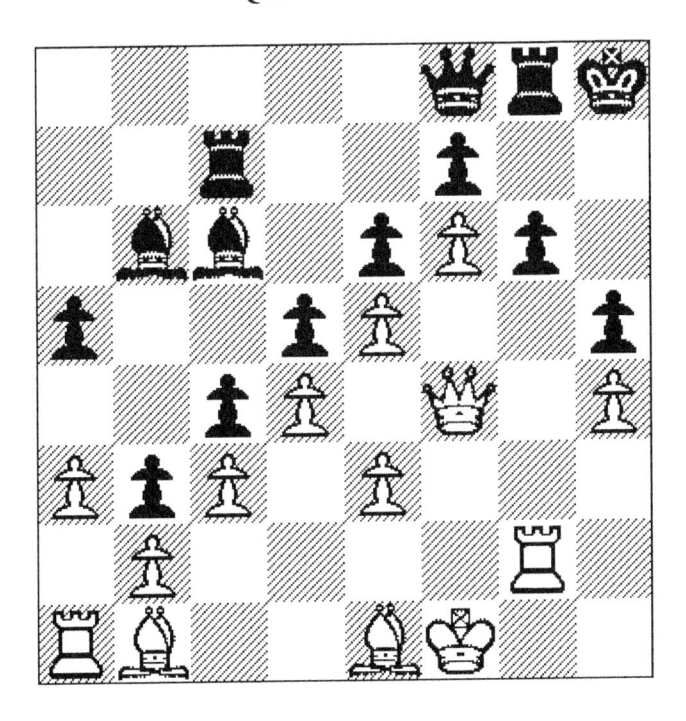

White has been threatening Bg3, Qg4, Bf4, Bg5, Qf4 and Bh6.

On 35...h6, a similar manoeuvre will happen, and black can not capture on g5, as it gets mated on the h file.

36. Qg5 a4 37. Bg3 Ra7 38. Bf4

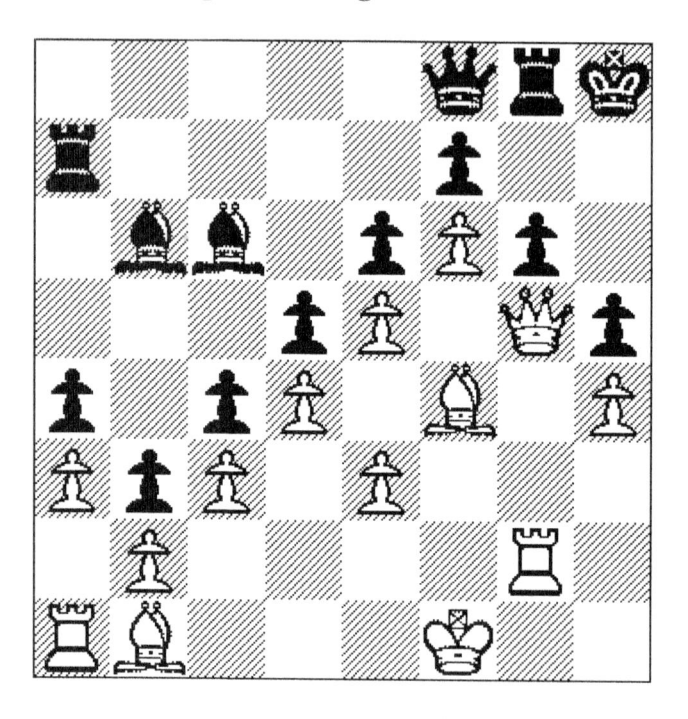

Part of the regrouping is completed, but still no mate in sight.

A continuation is necessary.

Rd7 39. Qg3 Bd8 40. Qf3 Ra7

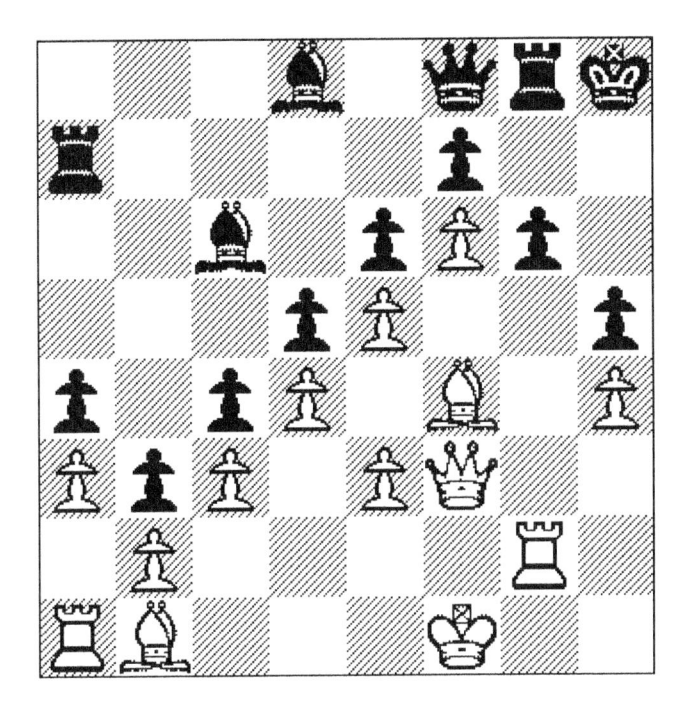

The queen has freed the g5 square, and now 41. Rg5! Qh6(otherwise, Rh5) 42. Rg6 Rg6 43. Bh6 Rh6 44. Qf4 was winning immediately.

41. Kf2

What a pity.

Rc7 42. Bg5 Rc8 43. Qf4

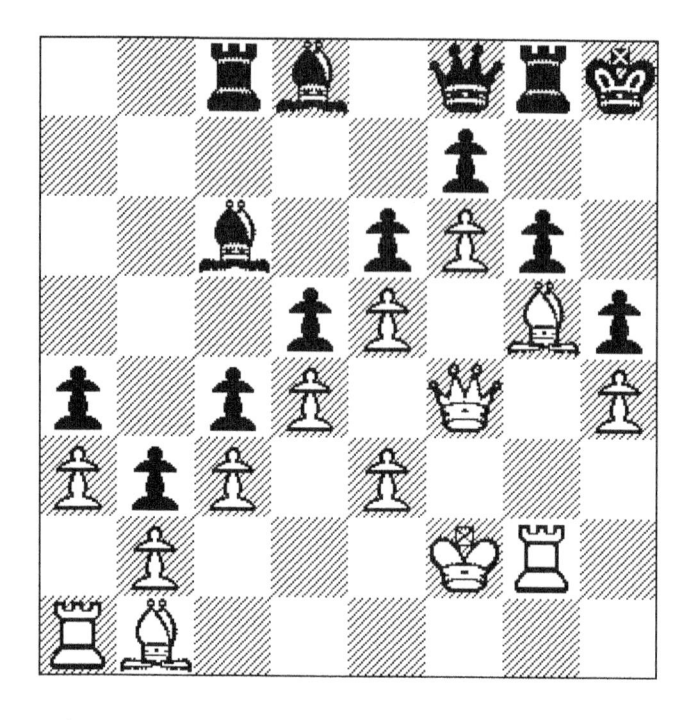

The position is always won, of course.

**Kh7 44. Qf3 Kh8 45. Bf4 Rc7
46. Ke2 Be8 47. Rg5**

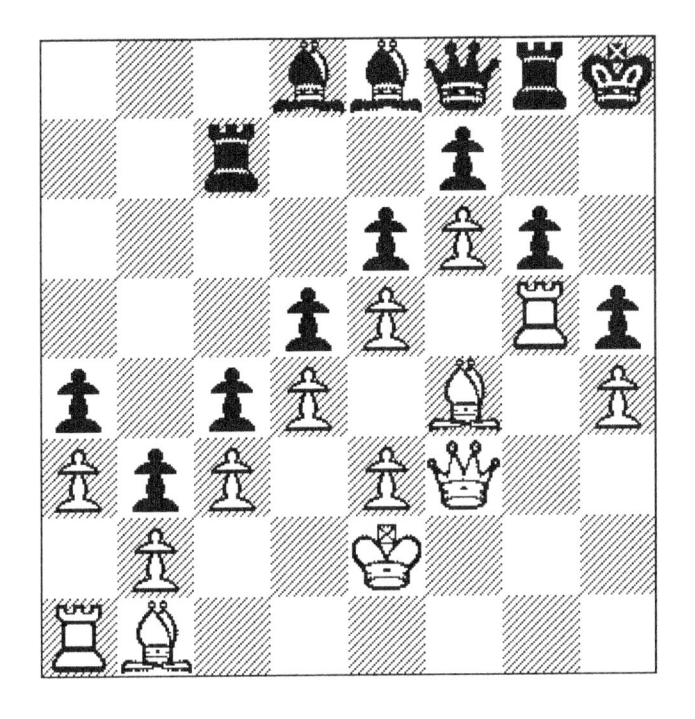

At last, I find the indicated manoeuvre.

Rg7

The engine sacs a rook.

**48. fg7 Qg7 49. Rg2 Rc8
50. Bg5 Bg5 51. Rg5**

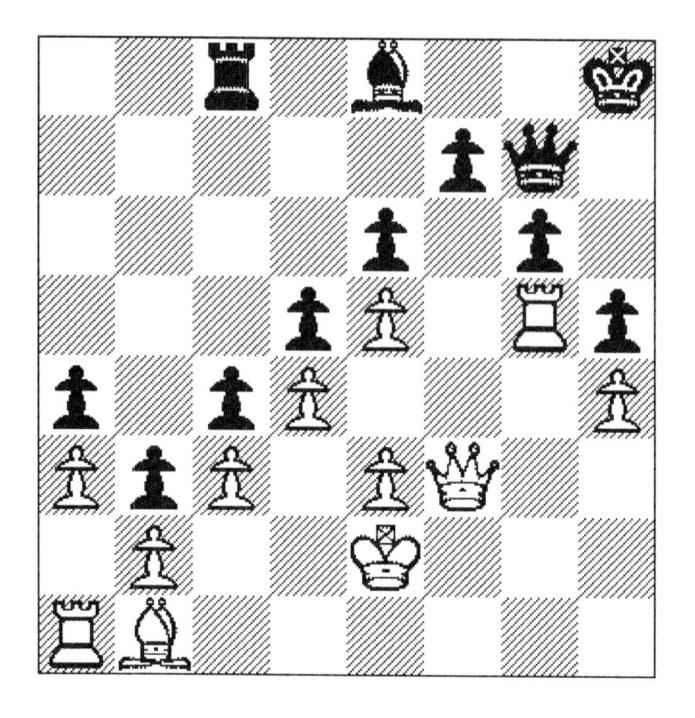

Stockfish resigned.

After Bg6 fg6 Rf1, black is hopeless.
e4 is even better, though.

Game 18
You are KIDding me

December 5th 2013
White: Lyudmil Tsvetkov
Black: Stockfish DD
A07 Reti Opening, King's Indian Attack

1. d3

Well, 1.d3 is a strong move, definitely stronger than 1.e3. Reason is that the d3 pawn could support the e4 friendly pawn, which is closer to the enemy king than a d4 pawn, that could be supported by an e3 pawn.

Not all players know that, though.

d5 2. Nf3 Nf6 3. g3

The King's Indian is in store.

Nc6 4. Bg2 e5 5. O-O Be7
6. Nc3 O-O 7. e4 d4

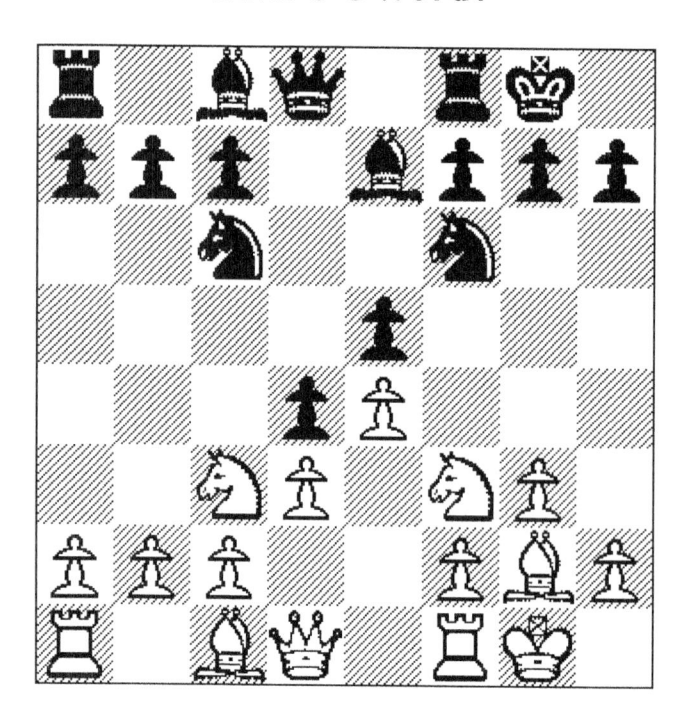

7...de4 8. de4 Qd1 9. Rd1 leads to small white advantage.

Maybe, this is the way to counter the KIA altogether.

Stockfish closes the center, but that perfectly suits white.

8. Ne2

The knight retreats, but towards the king side. It is important where your pieces are, even when retreating. The king side is always a preferable location, as pieces there are closer both to the enemy king, to attack it, and the own king, to lend it a helping hand in defence.

Bg4

Not a bad move, but not best either. 8...h6, to secure a place on e6 for the bishop(otherwise, on Be6 straight, white plays Ng5, followed by f4), might have been better, not wasting any time in development. Now, white can kick the bishop with a tempo.

9. h3 Be6

9...Bf3 10. Bf3 gives white the bishop pair, further increasing positional assets.

10. Kh1

The white king secures a place for the knight on f3 on g1, so that f2-f4 could be pushed. On g1, the knight will be also supporting the potentially weak h3 pawn, retreats to h2, d2 or e1 all seem more awkward.

Nd7

Black also kind of prepares an f7-f5 thrust.

11. Nfg1

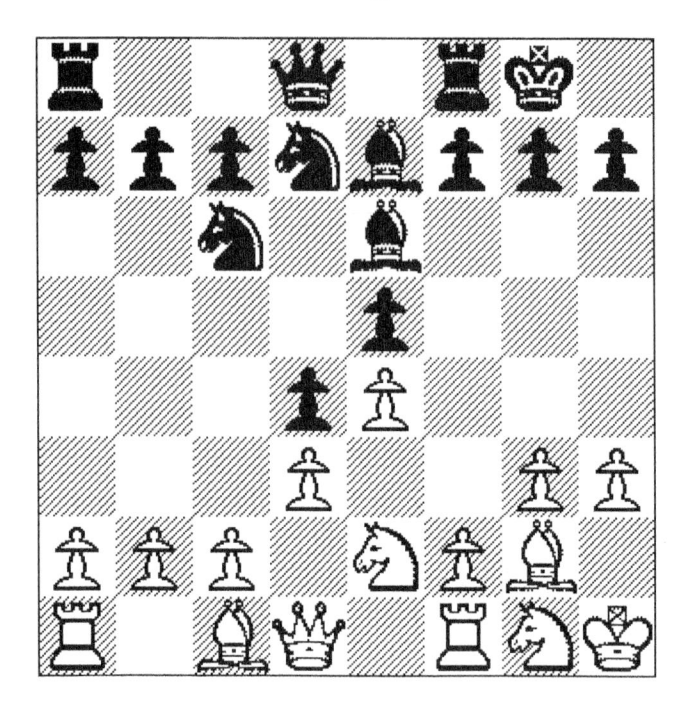

Now, f2-f4 is ready to go.

f6

Black would have loved to trade dark-square bishops with Bg5, but on that the opponent has f4 too.

The problem of black is that, due to specific positional nuances, it can not push f5, as after 11...f5 12. ef5 Bf5 13. g4!(Bc6 is weak, as after bc6 white has traded a strong bishop for a weak knight and simultaneously loosened its king shelter) Be6(Bg6 is hardly better) 14. Ng3, white places a strong outpost on e4, either knight or bishop, depending on circumstances, getting a sensible edge. So, Stockfish prepares for the incoming assault by strengthening its central foothold, the e5 square.

12. f4 Ncb8

Preparing c7-c5.

13. f5

A tempo-gaining move that simultaneously brings the f5 pawn closer to the enemy king. The center is closed and white has already extended a powerful c2-d3-e4-f5 pointed chain.

Bf7 14. g4

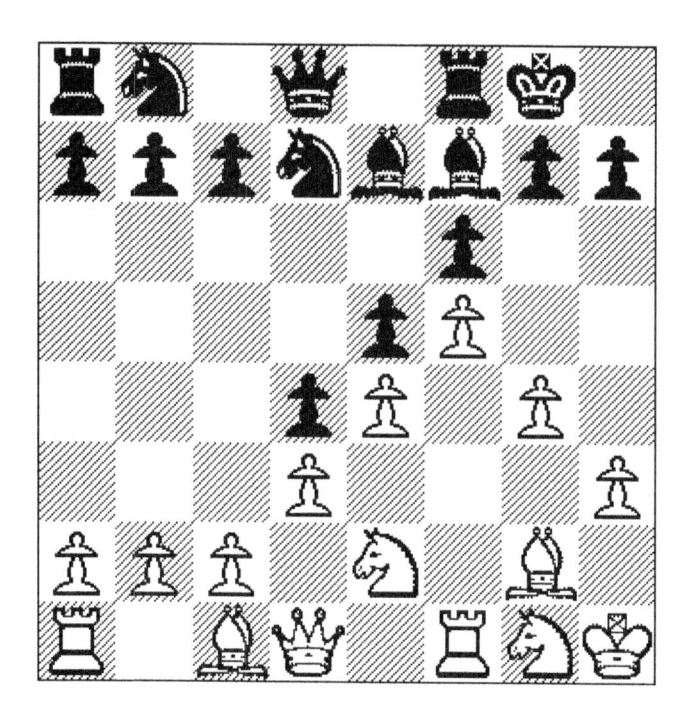

The outward appearance of the white pawn structure definitely appeals to me. White has also quite some space for its pieces to develop behind the advanced pawns.

c5

A timely counterthrust, with c5-c4 already a threat.

15. b3

Preventing c4.

Nc6

Stockfish is slow. 15...b5 16. a4 c4 17. ab5 cb3 18. cb3 Qb6 might have been the better choice.

16. h4

Aiming at g4-g5 and simultaneously freeing the h3 square for a friendly piece to occupy it. The bundled-up white pieces gradually start to unravel.

b5 17. Ng3

Closer to the enemy king.

c4

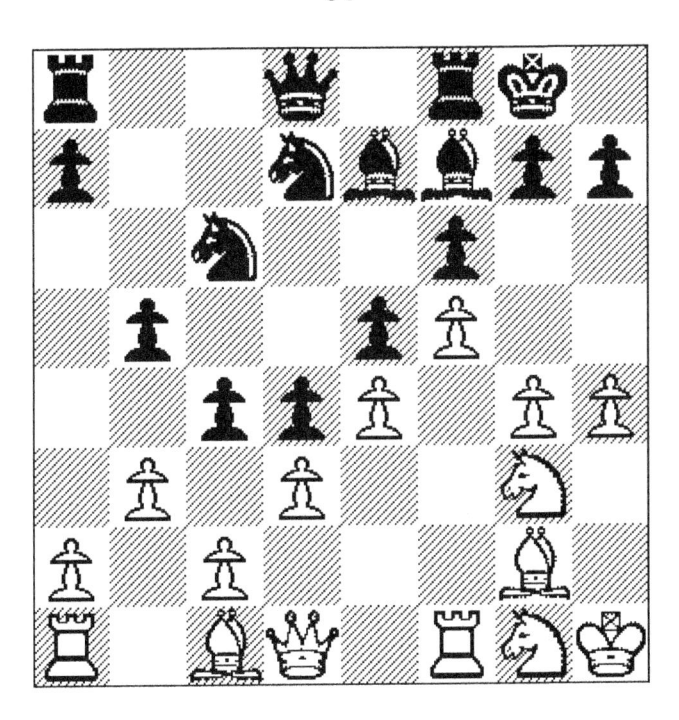

Well, this is a double-edged position, with white having an obvious edge due to its storming pawns being considerably closer to the enemy king.

18. Nf3

Emphasising development.
Of course, capturing on c4, opening the game on the queen side, only suits black.

Nc5

Pressuring more the d3 point.

19. g5

Both the knight on f3 and the bishop on c1 support the g5 square, so this push is now possible.

cd3

A correct decision. 19...c3 instead, although gaining considerable space, would be a tremendous positional mistake, closing the game on the queen side and leaving black devoid of counterplay.

20. cd3 Nb4

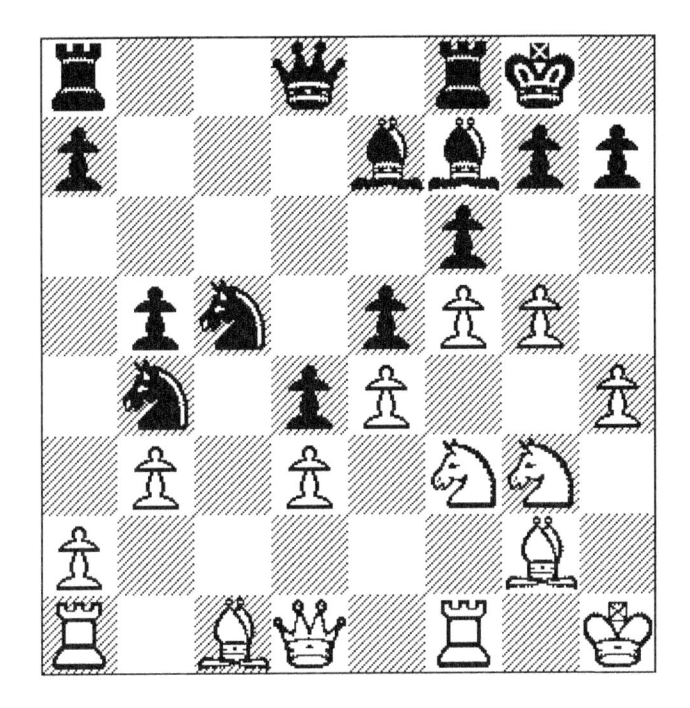

How should white defend the d3 pawn? Ne1 is not only too passive, but leaves the g5 pawn en prise. So, the only solution is to attack, no matter what.

21. g6!

Sacrificing a pawn, but breaking open the black king position and energy-charging the friendly pieces, which find excellent places on the spots previously occupied by white pawns.

hg6

Retreat is no option. On 21...Be8, 22. gh7, followed by h5(white can protect the d3 pawn with Ne1 before that, though), gives white significant advantage.

22. fg6

The f5 square is already free for the knight.

Bg6 23. h5!

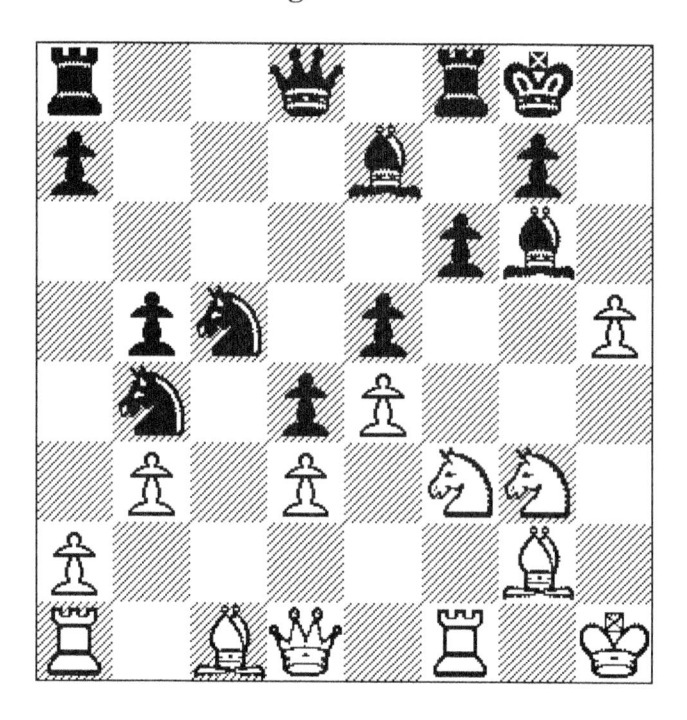

Gaining tempo first.

Bh7

The f5 square should be under control.

24. Nh4!

Taking aim at both g6 and f5, while clearing the way for the queen to g4.

Nbd3

24...Ncd3? 25. a3 Nc1 26. ab4, and the knight on c1 falls.

25. Ngf5

Qg4 is already a serious threat.

Nc1

25...Nf4 26. Qg4 Rf7 27. Nh6, and white wins at least the exchange.

26. Rc1

The rook develops towards the center.

Ne6

Envisaging to obstruct enemy attacks by posting the knight on either g5 or f4.
Simultaneously, the g7 point is defended.

27. Ng6!

Attacking the rook on f8 and the bishop on e7 at the same time, so one of them should fall.

27...Bg6, capturing the knight, is extremely dangerous, as after 28. hg6, followed by Qh5, white is threatening mate on h7 all the time.

Bb4

One way or another, the exchange is lost, so at least increase the activity of the bishop.

28. Qg4

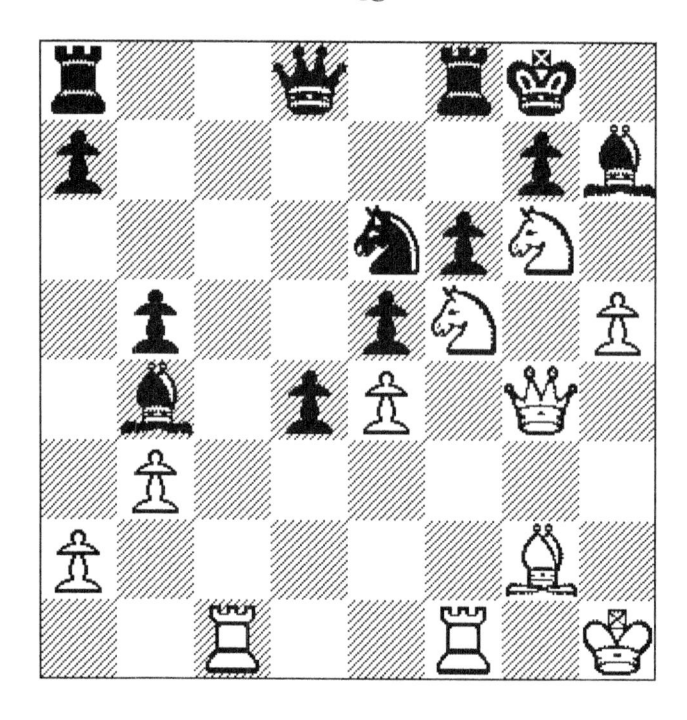

White is 2 pawns down, so 28. Nf8 Qf8, leaving black with the bishop pair and excellent minor posting opportunities on c3 and f4 is not acceptable at all. The right solution is an all-out attack. Nh6 check, followed by Qe6, picking up the enemy knight, will threaten in different variations.

Bg6

Black should have played Ng5, covering the g file, though even in this case after 29. Nf8 Bf8(Qf8 Rc7) 30. Rc6, the gorgeously positioned knight on f5 plus control over the open c file ensure white much preferable chances.

28...Bd2, on the other hand, seems quite dangerous due to 29. Nf8 Qf8 30. Rc6(30...Qe8 31. Re6! Qe6 32. Nh6 check, winning the queen on e6), but 29. Nfe7(the black bishop has left the e7 square unprotected) Kf7 30. Rc6 is also possible and should be amenable to sophisticated tactics on the part of white, though I have not checked that with a machine to be certain.

29. hg6 Ng5 30. Qh5

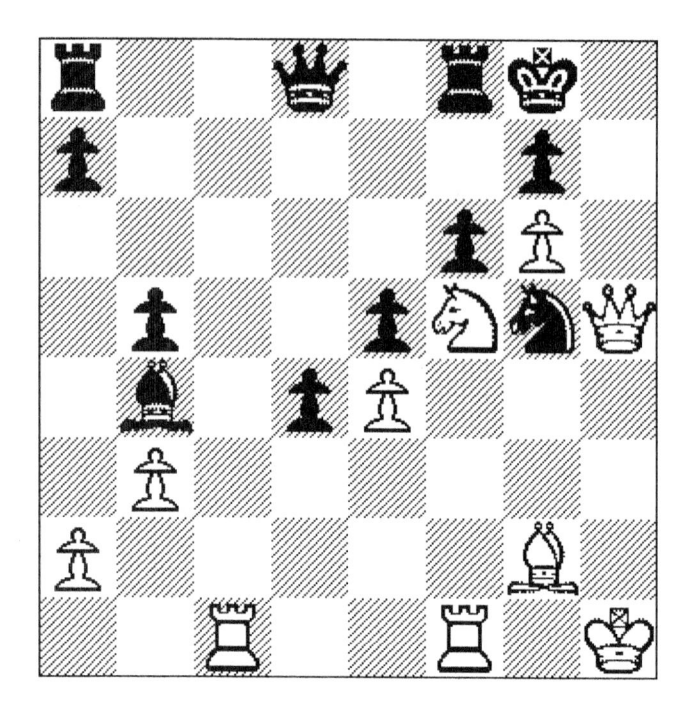

Now, as soon as the black knight on g5 is removed, white mates on h7. It is hard to believe black can save that in any imaginable machine way, though Stockfish resists for another 15 moves.

Rc8

Stockfish wants to exchange pieces to decrease the amount of threats.

31. Bf3!

Clearing the g2 square for the white king and threatening Kg2 and Rh1 with mate on h8.

Qa5

Simply no other alternatives.

d3-d2 advance is too slow, while 31...Bd2(Rc1 Rc1 Bd2 leads to the same outcome) 32. Rc8 Qc8 33. Rg1 Re8 34. Rg5! Bg5 35. Qh7 Kf8 36. Qh8 mates.

32. a4

Well, more convincing was 32. Rc8 Rc8 33. Rg1 Ba3(to give the queen the opportunity to check on e1) 34. Rg5 Rc1 35. Rg1 Rg1 36. Kg1 Qe1 37. Kg2 Qd2 38. Kh3 and the king escapes eternal check.

Ba3

The rook is attacked and the queen would like to d2.

33. Ra1

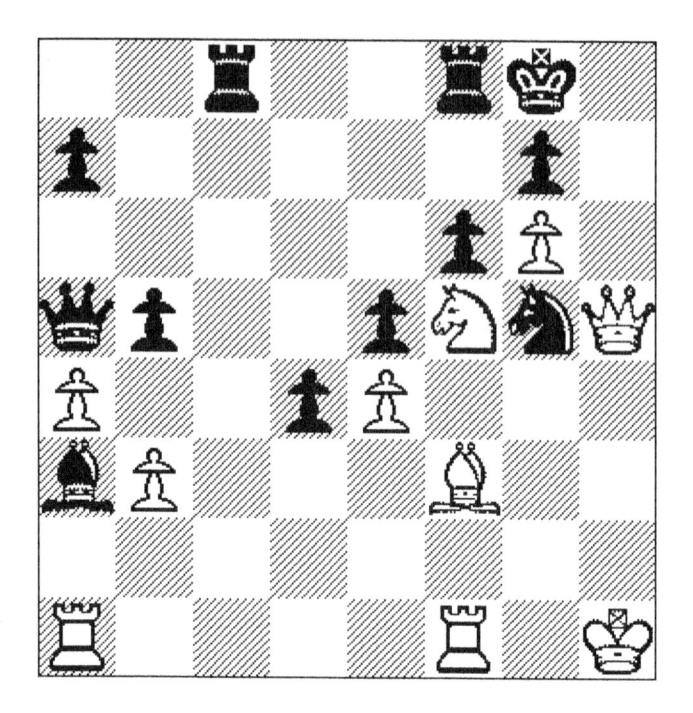

Attacking the black bishop in turn.

Qc3

Well, nothing better.
33...Bc5 34. Rg1
33...Bb2/b4?? 34. Ne7 mate

34. Ra3 Rc7

What to do.

35. Ra2

After the white rook reaches h2, it is all over.

Qd3

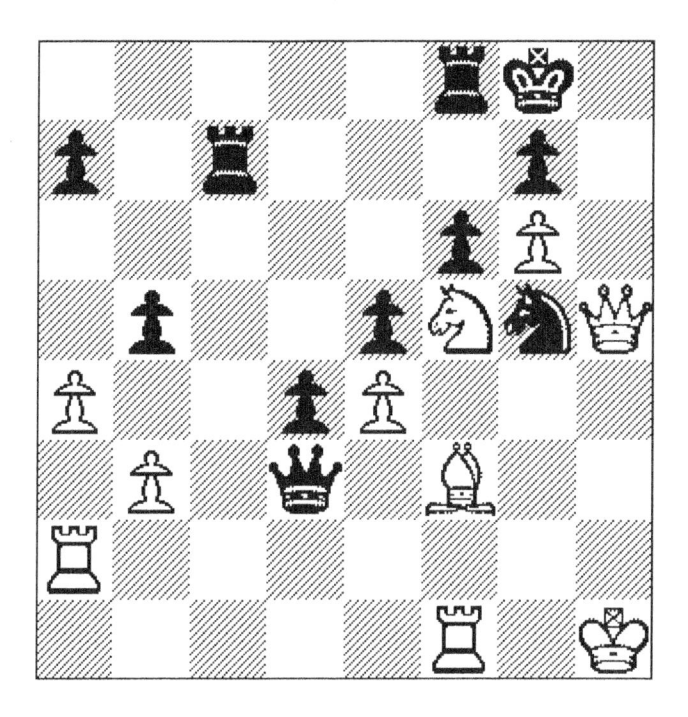

Threatening Qf1 check.

36. Kg1

The king defends the rook.
Still not too late to blunder, especially in a faster game.

36. Rg1 Qf3
36. Rff2 Rc1
36. Bg4 Qe4

Re8 37. Rh2

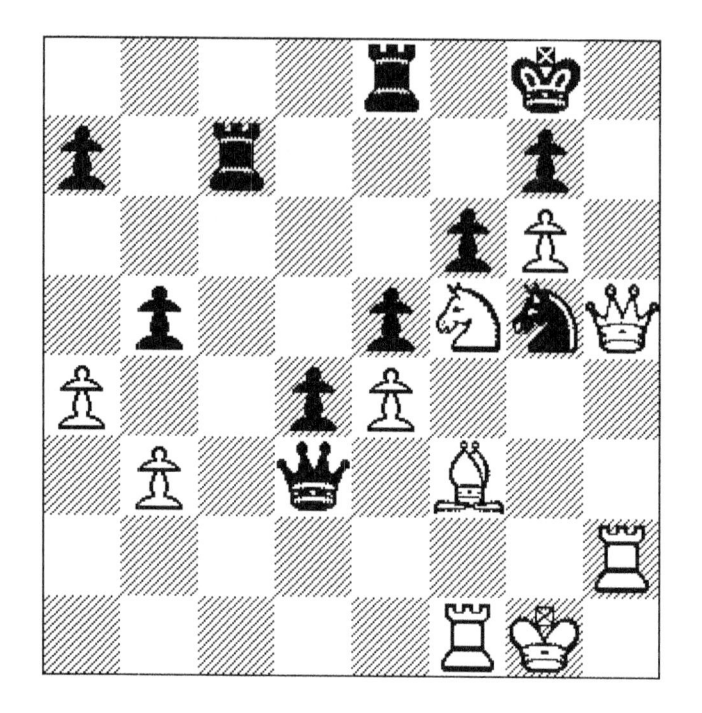

Well, that is the end of it.

Nf3 38. Qf3 Qf3 39. Rf3 Rc1 40. Rf1

40. Kg2 Rc2, one of the rooks gets changed, so no quick mate after doubling on h8.

Rc7 41. Rh7 ba4 42. ba4 Rec8 43. Kg2

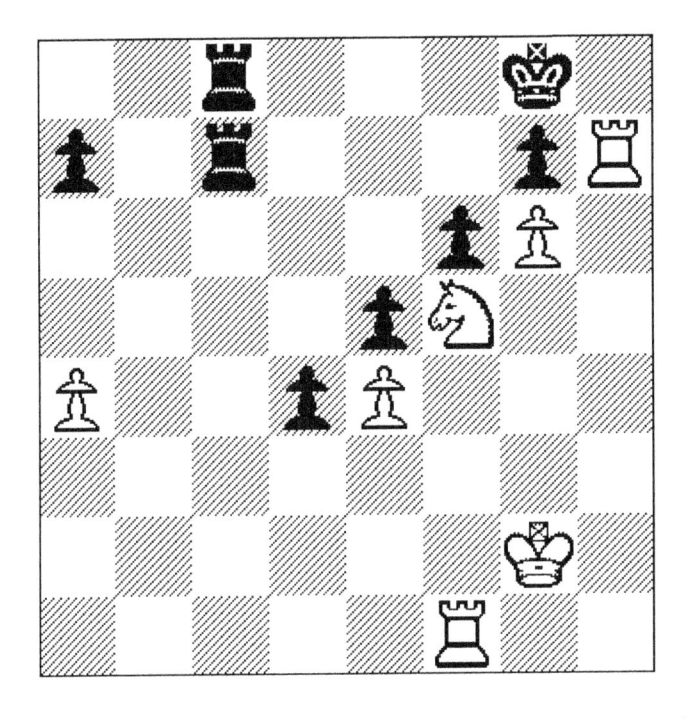

This is extremely easy to win, it just takes couple of moves more.

Rc2 44. Rf2 Rf2 45. Kf2 Rc7 46. Nh6

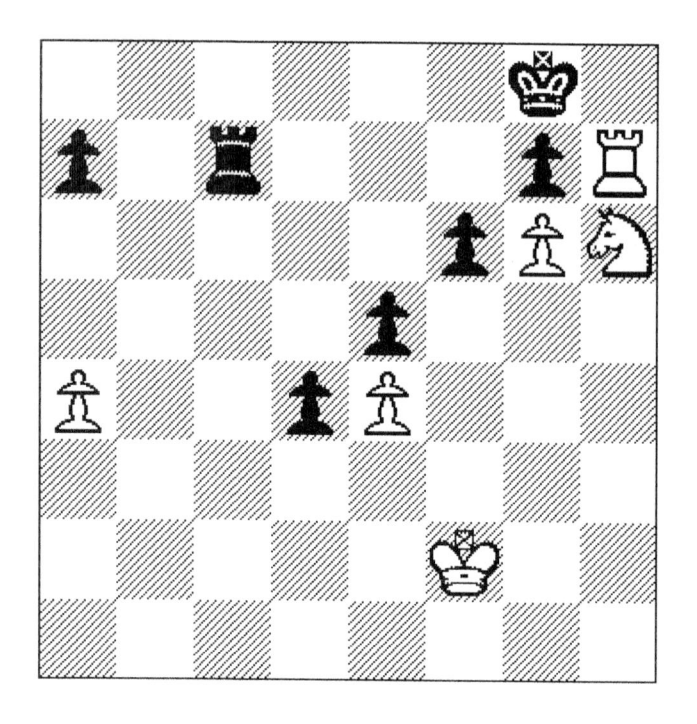

Stockfish resigned.

46...Kf8 47. Rh8 Ke7 48. Nf5 Ke6 49. Re8 Kd7 50. Re7 Kd8 51. Rc7 Kc7 52. Ng7

Game 19
No chance

December 5th 2013
White: Lyudmil Tsvetkov
Black: Stockfish DD
A07 Reti Opening, King's Indian Attack

1. d3 d5 2. Nf3 Nc6 3. g3 e5 4. Bg2 Nf6 5. O-O Be7 6. Nc3 O-O 7. e4 d4 8. Ne2 Qd6 9. h3

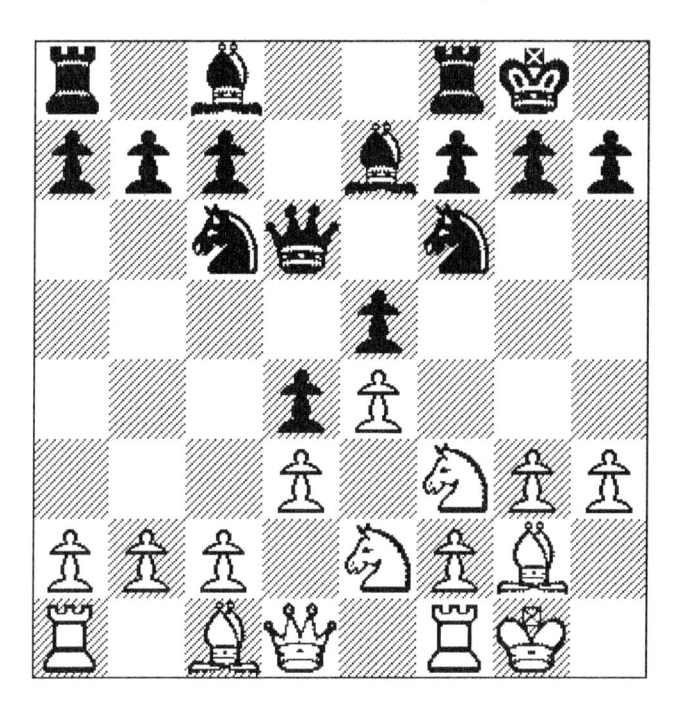

A repeat of the Reti-King's Indian Attack. This time, white does not even allow Bg4.

a5

Stockfish starts an early counterthrust.

10. Kh1

Same idea, the g1 square is promptly evacuated for the f3 knight.

a4

The engine aims at a4-a3.

11. a3!

Of course, a4 should not be allowed.
If black manages to push a3, then both ba3 and b3 are bad.
a3 ba3 Qd8(the bishop on e7 targets now the a3 pawn), and the a3 pawn falls, leaving black with significant positional advantage in terms of much superior pawn structure.
a3 b3 is no good, although the queen side gets closed, as the advanced a3 pawn, coupled with its advanced friend on d4, greatly restrict the activity of a large portion of the white pieces.
a3 also takes under control the b4 square, that is a possible penetration point for the opponent.

Nd7 12. Nfg1 f6 13. f4 Nc5 14. f5

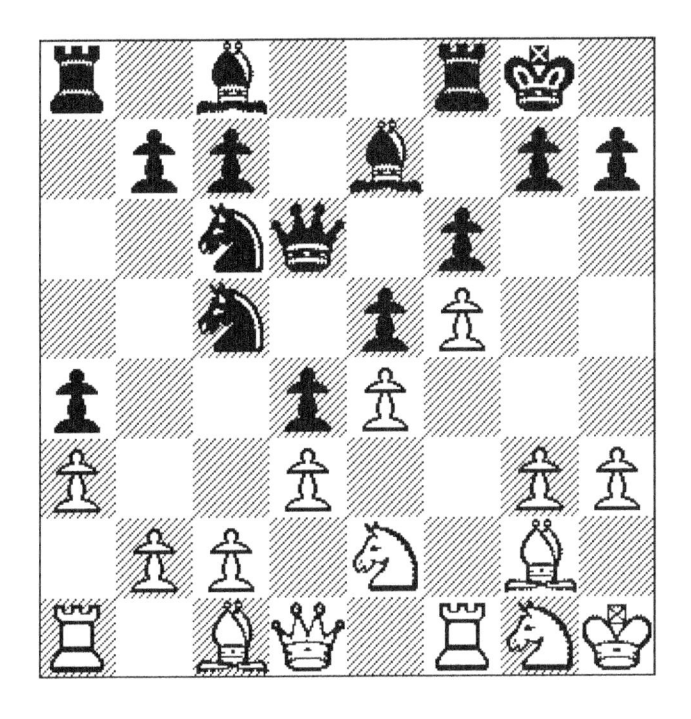

Plans are clear: white will attack on the king side, black will try to counter on the queen side.

b6

Stockfish intends to develop its light-square bishop on the long diagonal, but 14...b5 straight, to break sooner with b5-b4 and more active counterplay, was doubtless a preferred solution.

Similar small inaccuracies frequently decide games.

15. g4 Bb7 16. h4

White does not lose any time in attack management.

Nd8

Freeing the diagonal for the b7 bishop, that now also attacks the vital e4 square, but also envisaging Nf7, to attempt stopping the advance of the g4 storming pawn to g5.

On c6, one way or another, the knight has nothing to do, too immobile, while transferring it to a5 is also completely useless, as both the b3 and c4 penetration squares are safely guarded by opponent pawns.

17. Ng3 Nf7 18. Nf3

The knight supports a future g5 thrust.

The white pieces slowly develop behind the central wall of blocked pawns.

Qd8

Adding another x-ray attack to the g5 point, so that g4-g5 is still currently impossible.

19. Rg1!

Lining up the rook on the same file as the enemy king and simultaneously pinpointing the g5 square to support the advance of the white pawn.

Nd7

The e4 point is a hopeless enterprise(the knight on g3 defends it too), so Stockfish decides to bring one minor piece more closer to its own king for the purposes of defence. At the same time, a c7-c5 counterthrust is prepared.

20. Bh3!

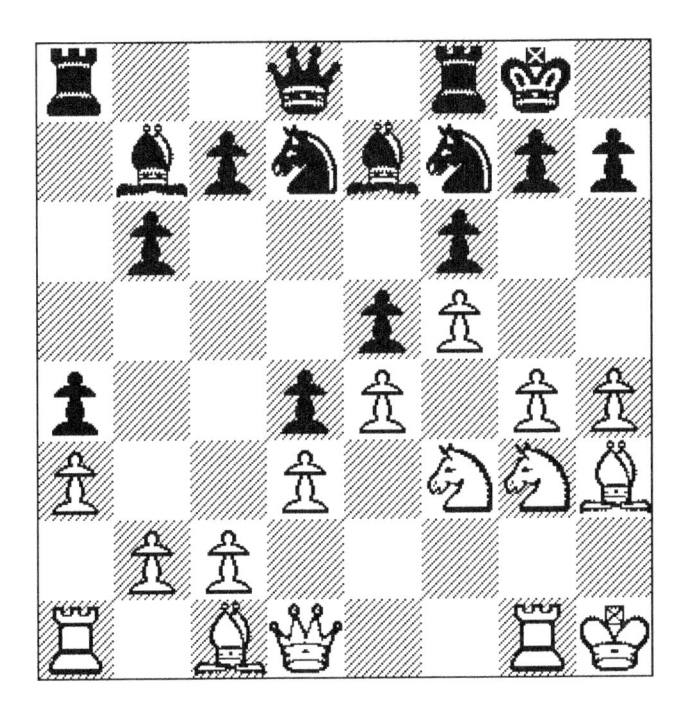

A good move.

Clearing the g file for the rook, x-ray-attacking the d7 knight and improving the position of the bishop.

h6

Well, this is hardly a mistake, as the position is certainly already lost for black.

Nh5, followed by g5, has been threatening. By playing h6, Stockfish adds another controller of the g5 square, but simultaneously weakens the g6 point.

One way or another, white's advantage is so big in positional terms, that sooner or later it will manage to break through with g5, either after regrouping, or due to readily available tactical motifs.

21. Nh5

Attacks g7 and clears the g file for the rook.

Nc5

Targeting the e4 square.

White should be careful, as otherwise various sac moves on e4 could be quite unpleasant and even fully turn the tables. We should not forget, that the b7 bishop is lined up against the white king, and the central roll of black pawns, if left free, could become quite dangerous.

22. Qe2

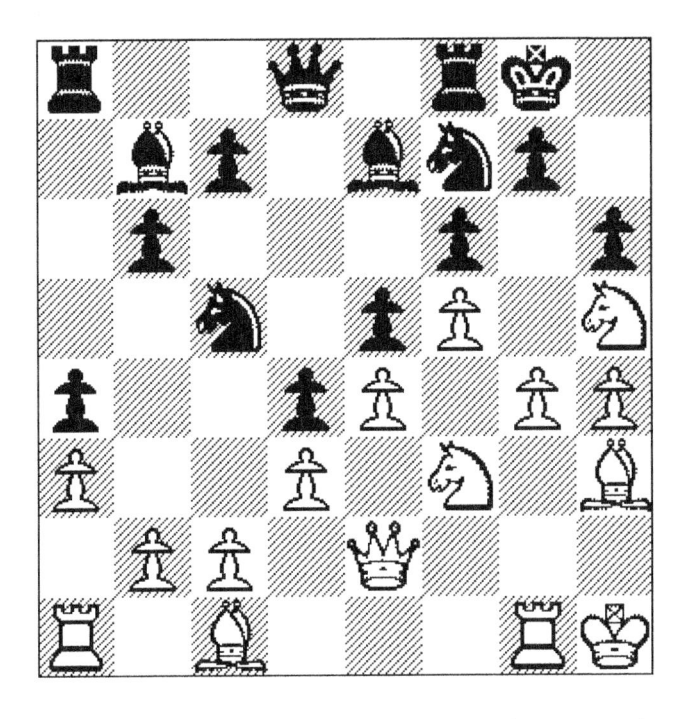

Taking the e4 square under control, preventing any possible surprise sacrifices.

Look at this position: black is completely helpless. The advanced black pawns on a4 and d4 are safely blocked, there are no levers in sight to open the game on the queen side, while on the king side white has thrashing advantage.

Never give a single chance to the engine, and you are going to win against it.

Bc6

Improving the location of the bishop. At some point, it might be suited for a transfer to e8, where it will challenge the white knight on h5.

23. Bd2

Completing development, taking under control the b4 square(so that a possible b5-b4 push is firmly neutralised) and intending to double rooks on the g file.

Ra7

Preparing to place the queen on a8 to attack the e4 square once more. In the current situation, black's only hope is some tactical antics.

24. Rg2

Freeing the g1 square for the rook on a1 to double.

Qa8

We guessed rightly, Stockfish attacks e4.

25. Re1!

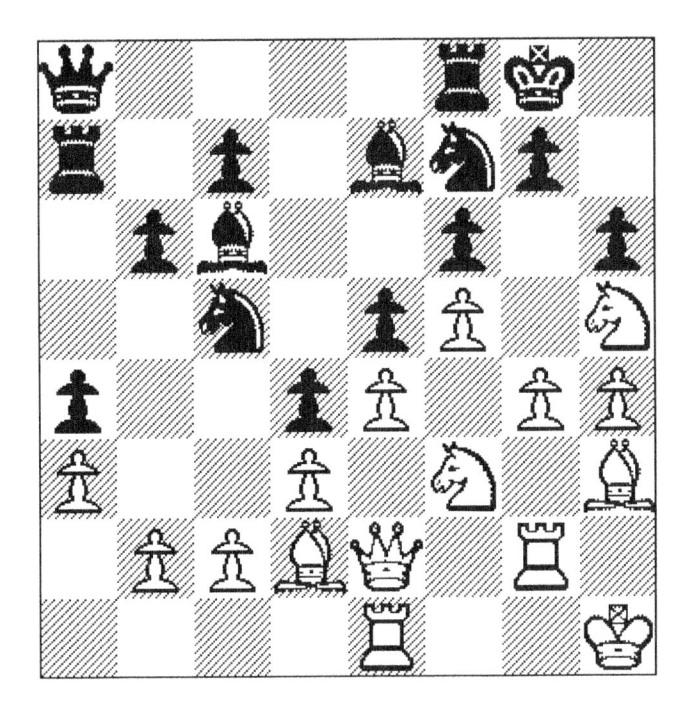

Prophylaxis!

25. Rg1 instead might constitute a fatal mistake, as after 25...Ne4! 26. de4 Be4, the white knight on f3, rook on g2 and king on h1 are all lined up against the queen-rook tandem on the long diagonal, and white could even lose.

The ensuing lines are complicated, but it is not necessary to check each and every ramification, when white has much better.

Nd6

Stockfish insists to take on e4.

Now, 26. g5? hg5 27. hg5 fg5 28. Ng5 Bg5(the knight on g5 has been guarding e4 too) 29. Bg5 Nde4! is extremely dangerous and mostly in the realm of engine-like play, so white must find a better move.

26. Ng3!

Defending e4 once more. On the next move, white will already push g5.

Qe8

The queen has nothing to do on a8 any more, so it comes closer to its king to defend it.
Good moves are difficult to see.

27. g5

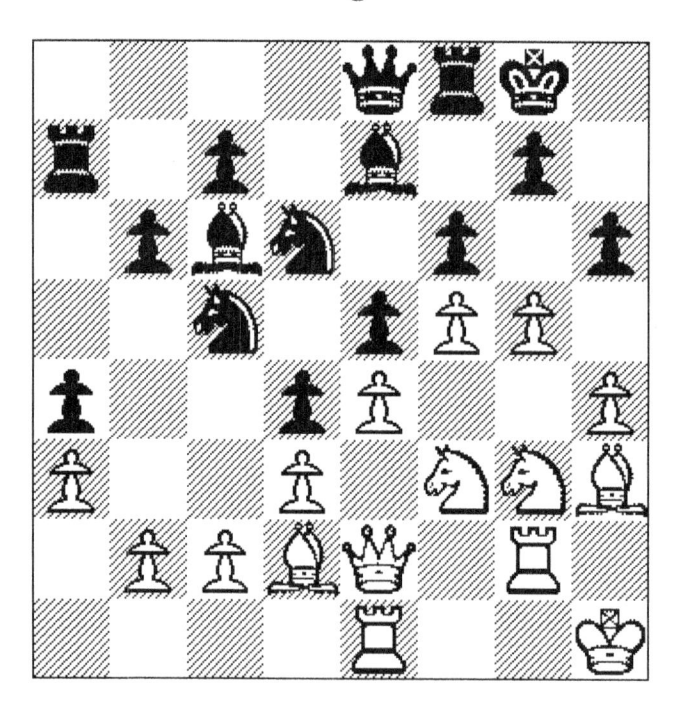

At last. So much preparation for such a simple push.

Black is doomed.

fg5

Otherwise, either gh6, g6, followed by Nh2, Qh5, Ng4 and a sac on h6, or Bg4-h5-g6 seal it.

28. hg5 Bg5 29. Ng5 hg5 30. Bg5

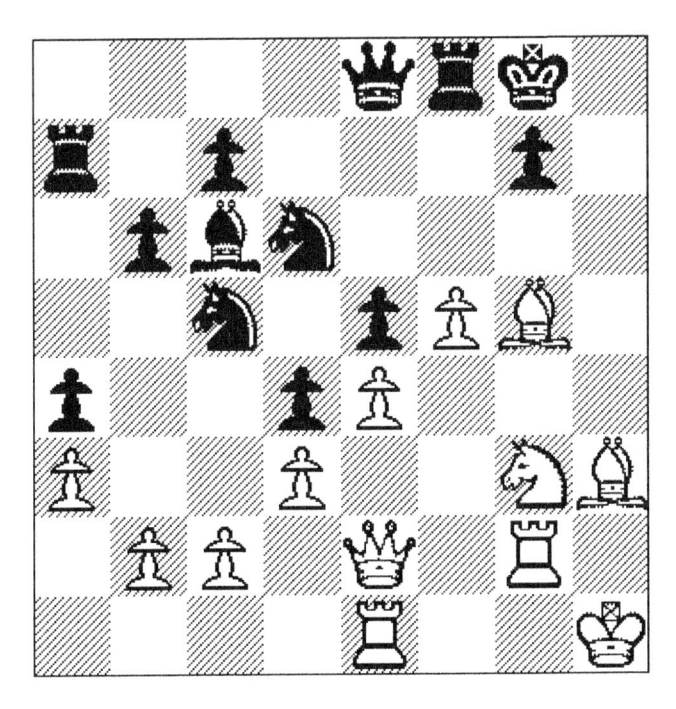

A forced exchange leaves black completely helpless.

Bg4-h5 threatens.

Rf7

Stockfish defends g7 once more.

31. Bg4

Proceeding according to plan.

Nd7 32. Bh5 Kf8 33. Rh2

Losing the exchange is black's smallest problem.

Nf6 34. Bg6

Everything wins here, but white threatens an immediate Rh8 Ng8 Bh7.

Ke7

Avoiding the nasty rook check.

35. Rh7

Going to the 7th.
The rook is safe, as the knight on f6 is pinned.

Qf8

35...Kd7 36. Bf6(other continuations are possible too) gf6 37. Bf7 Nf7 38. Qh5 makes no difference.

36. Nh5

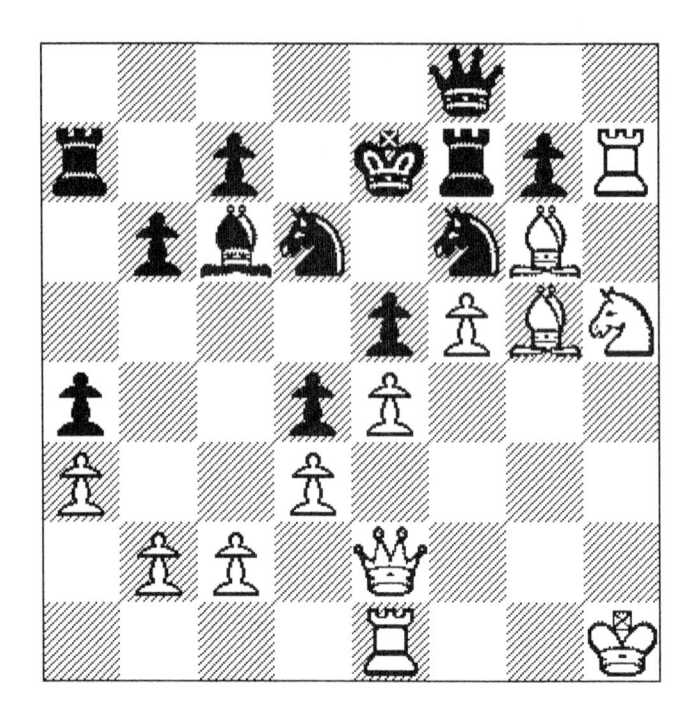

Black is completely stuck. One might think I have been playing black and Stockfish white.

Kd8 37. Nf6

Not that much a capturing move, rather than freeing the h5 square for the white queen.

Rf6

37...gf6 38. Bf7 Nf7(fg5 Qh5) 39. Bf6

38. Qh5

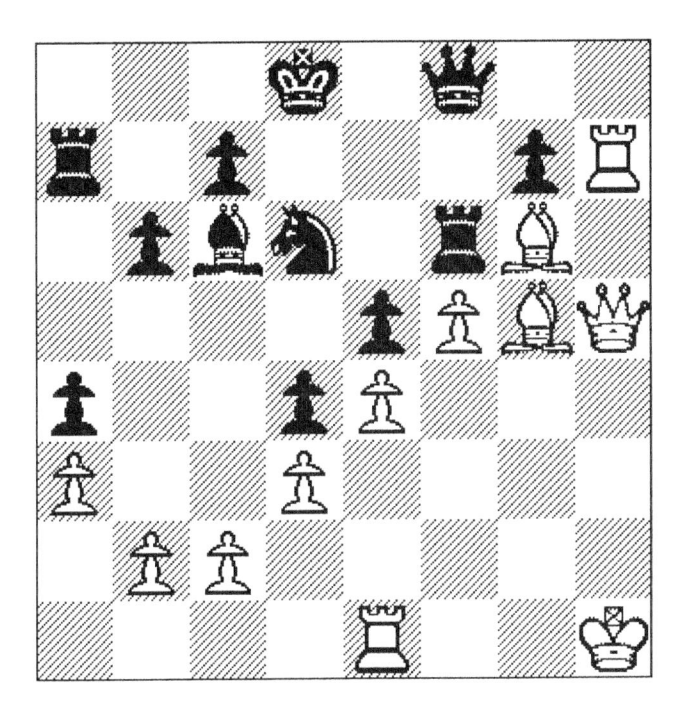

The threat of Rh8 is unavoidable.

1-0

Game 20
The powerful Torre

December 17th 2013
White: Lyudmil Tsvetkov
Black: Stockfish DD
A46 Queen's Pawn Game, Torre Attack

1. d4 Nf6 2. Nf3 e6 3. Bf4 Be7 4. e3

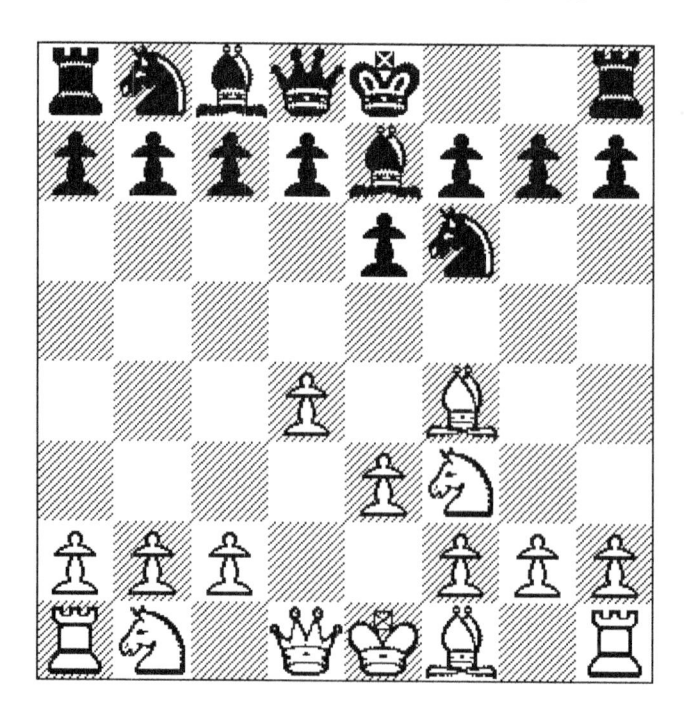

The Torre Attack is another excellent way to get a promising closed position against the top engines. The distinction to the King's Indian Attack is that white has a c3-d4-e5 more central pointed chain instead of d3-e4-f5 one.

Nh5

Attacking the bishop. Bishops are on average more valuable than knights, so nothing special could be said against that move.

5. Bg3

The bishop retreats to g3.

Bd3 instead is not very good, as after Nf4 ef4 d5, followed by 0-0 and c5, the white central pawn on d4 could be defended by a single pawn, c3, and becomes weak.

O-O

Black castles first.
The bishop on g3 has nowhere to go.

6. Bd3

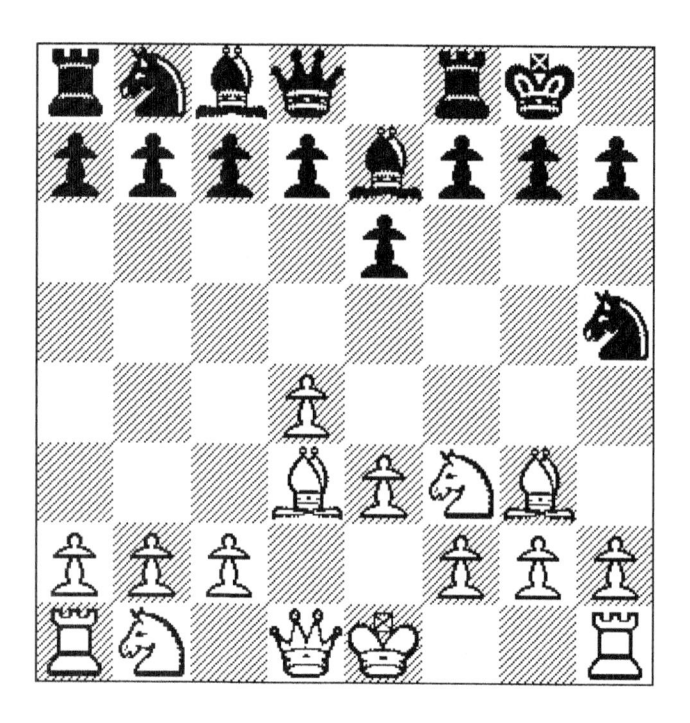

That bishop is very strong behind the wall of dark-square positioned pawns. For such a bishop, it is not regrettable to sacrifice the minor exchange.

d6

Not a bad move.

Stockfish might want to push e5, after for example Nc6 and Ng3 have been played(with h6 or g6 included, to avoid the check on h7). A pawn on e5 is always stronger than a pawn on d5.

6...d5 straight was an alternative, maybe even slightly better in the present circumstances.

7. O-O c5

Stockfish challenges the d4 pawn, but that is inconsequent.

Nc6, followed by Ng3 and e5, was certainly the better choice.

8. c3

Defending d4 a second time. It is always good to secure your central strong points.

Nd7

It is not very clear what Stockfish does with this one. Maybe, it wanted to transfer the knight to f6, when the other knight captures on g3, but that is too slow.

Nc6 was much better again.

When engines get an unfamiliar position, they start blundering on each and every move, just like humans.

9. Nbd2

c3 is inaccessible, but d2 is an excellent square for the knight too.

Ng3

Stockfish should capture at some point.

10. hg3 d5

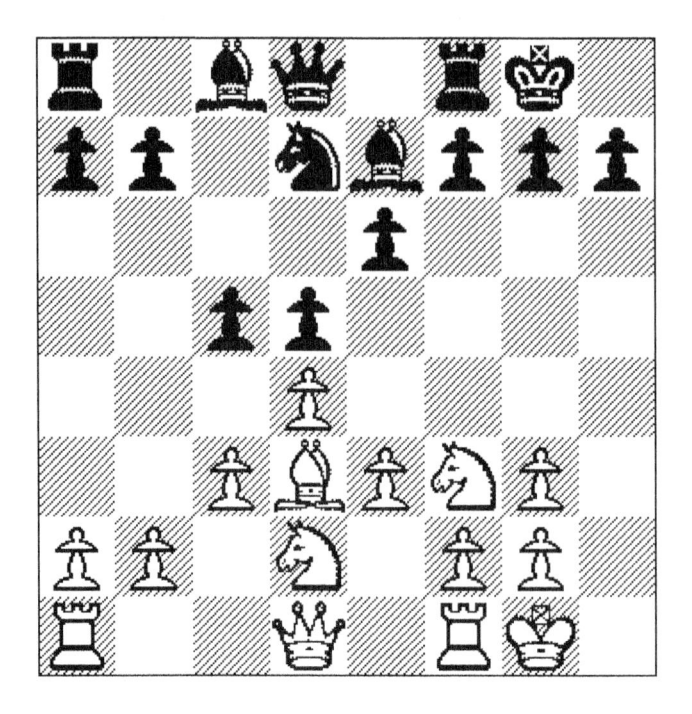

Well, you see now why Nd7 was a considerable inaccuracy. Stockfish has pushed the pawn to d5 in 2 intervals instead of one.

e6-e5 was awkward, as the knight is badly placed and limits the mobility of the bishop on c8 too.

11. Qe2

Simple development.

c4?

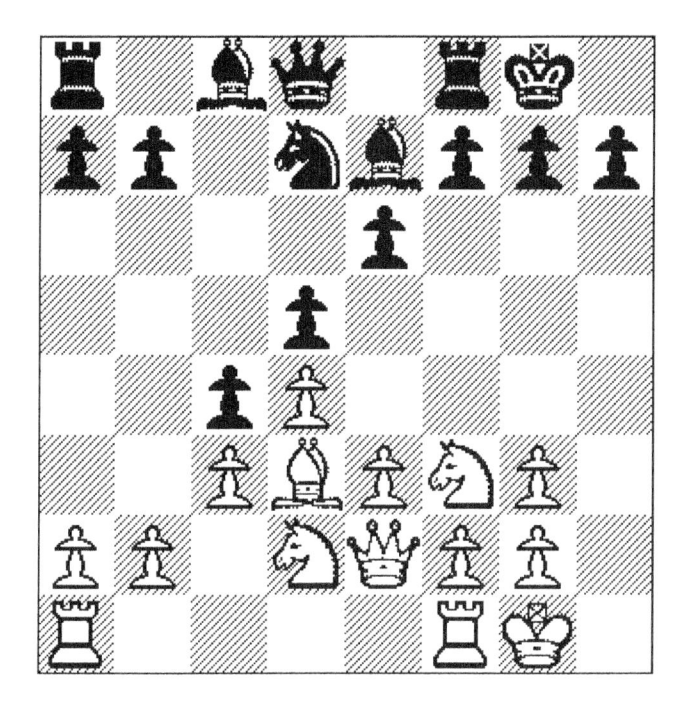

This is already a major positional mistake. Not the move itself, but the plan associated with it. Stockfish intends to attack on the queen side, but it forgets about its king side.

This move closes the game on the queen side, while the king side remains open to attacks. 11...f5 instead was definitely to prefer, restricting the e4 square, and white has nothing better than 12. Nh2(to push f4), followed by f4 and Nhf3, with only a small advantage.

12. Ne5 or 12. g4 are hardly better.

12. Bc2 b5

Stockfish should have played f5 again.

13. a3

Stopping b5-b4.

a5 14. e4

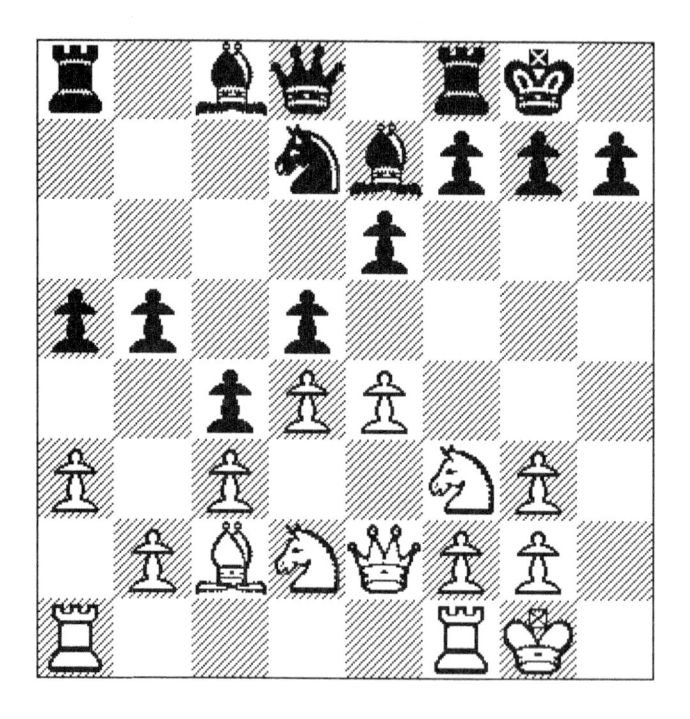

As the engine has not played f5, white breaks in the center with e4.

Now, de4 Qe4 loses the rook on a8 due to the mate threat on h7, while Nf6 e5 is simply bad.

Bb7

Stockfish develops, further challenging the e4 pawn.

15. e5!

That is the right solution.

White extends a powerful b2-c3-d4-e5 pointed chain towards the enemy king, increases the attacking range of the c2 bishop, with the e5 pawn severely pressuring the black king shelter all the time.

Attempting f7-f5 now is inadequate, as after ef6 Rf6(otherwise e6 simply falls) Ng5(attacking both h7 and e6) Nf8 f4, followed by Rae1, the e6 pawn is extremely weak.

Nb6 16. Nh2

Preparing f4.

Bc6

Stockfish starts shuffling.
16...b4 might have been better, but white retains quite some edge after that too.

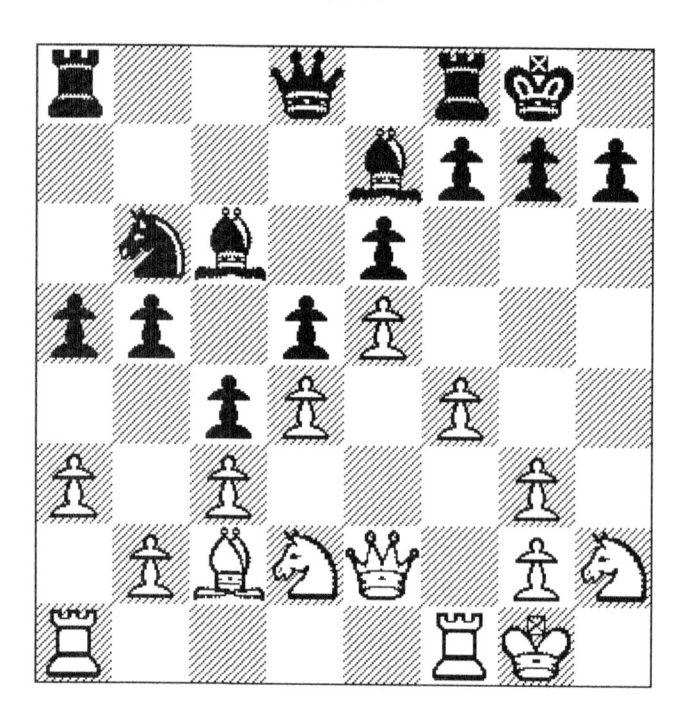

17. f4

The white pawn structure looks powerful, does not it?

That is why I like closed games with longer chains of pawns.

Qe8

Possibly, to trade light-square bishops after b5-b4 and Ba4 is played, but also defending the e6 pawn in a range of variations.

18. g4!

Doubled, but strong.

The g4 pawn heads to g5 to completely paralyse the black king shelter.

18. f5 is much weaker, as after 18...ef5(otherwise white pushes the pawn to f6) 19. Bf5 g6, followed by Bg5-h6, black is quite fine.

18. Qh5 f5 is even worse, as the attacking line of the white bishop is covered and the queen on h5 simultaneously assaulted.

b4

At last, Stockfish starts active counterplay.

19. g5

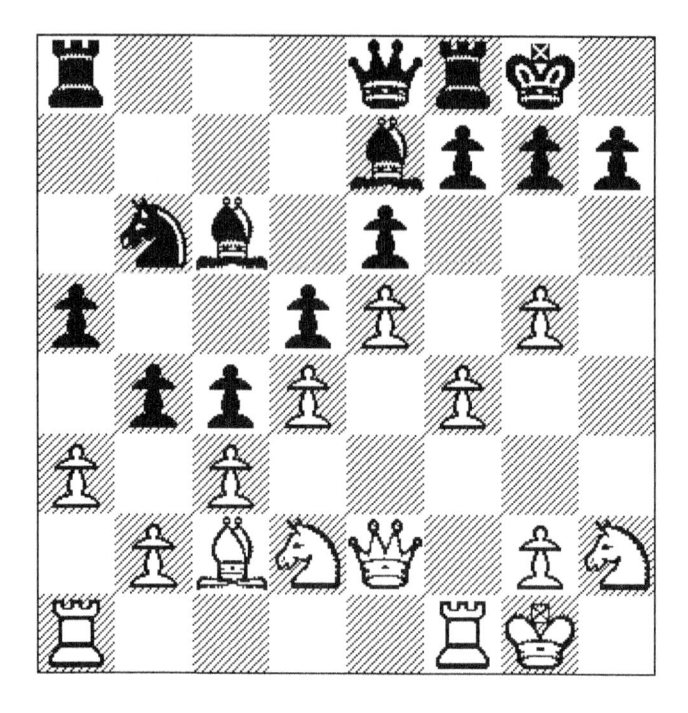

Ng4, but also different tactics, like Rf3, followed by Bh7 and Rh3, already threaten.

But not Qh5 f5.

Na4

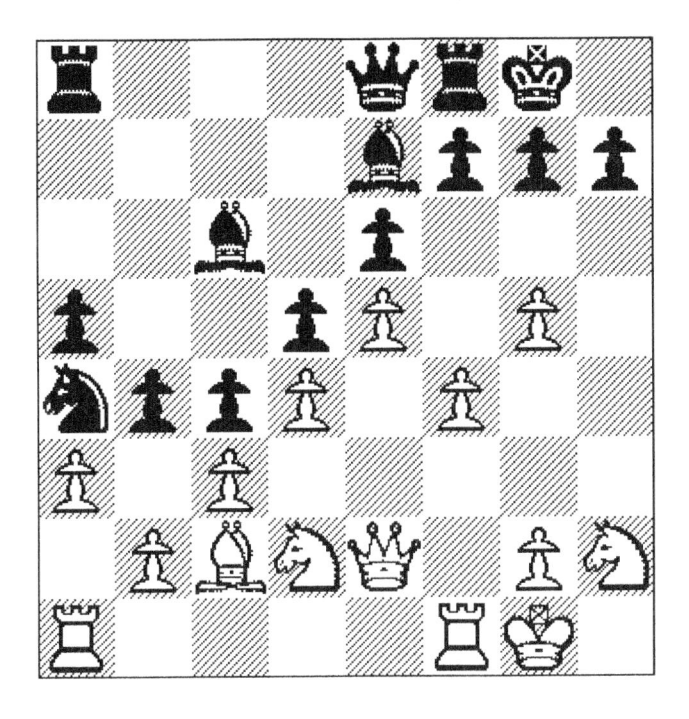

19...Ba4, b3, bc3 or ba3 basically changes nothing.

19...f5 is impossible, because after ef6, the queen picks the e6 pawn with check.

20. Ng4

Not a bad move, but white misses 20. Bh7! check Kh7 21. Qh5 Kg8 22. Rf3, with mate(f6 g6, g6 Qh6 and Rh3).

bc3 21. Nf6

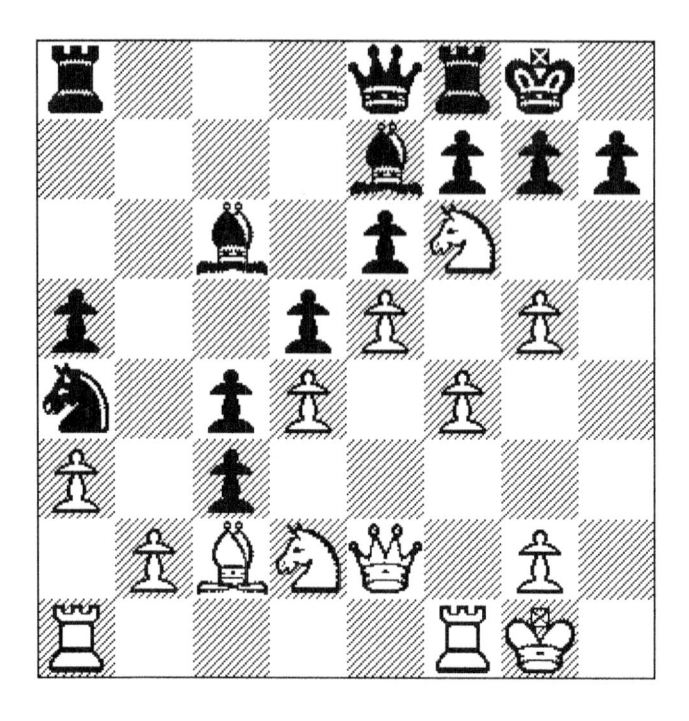

The position is funny, that is why I am posting it. It is impossible to avoid mate, in the short, or a bit longer term.

Bf6

gf6 gf6, followed by Qh5, loses even quicker.

22. gf6 g6 23. Qg4

To continue with Qg5 and Qh6.

cb2

23...Kh8 or cd2 instead does not save the game, of course, as white has simply too much firepower concentrated on the king side.

24. Qh4 Kh8

In order for the rook to defend the g7 square.
24...h5 25. Qg5 Kh7 26. Qh5

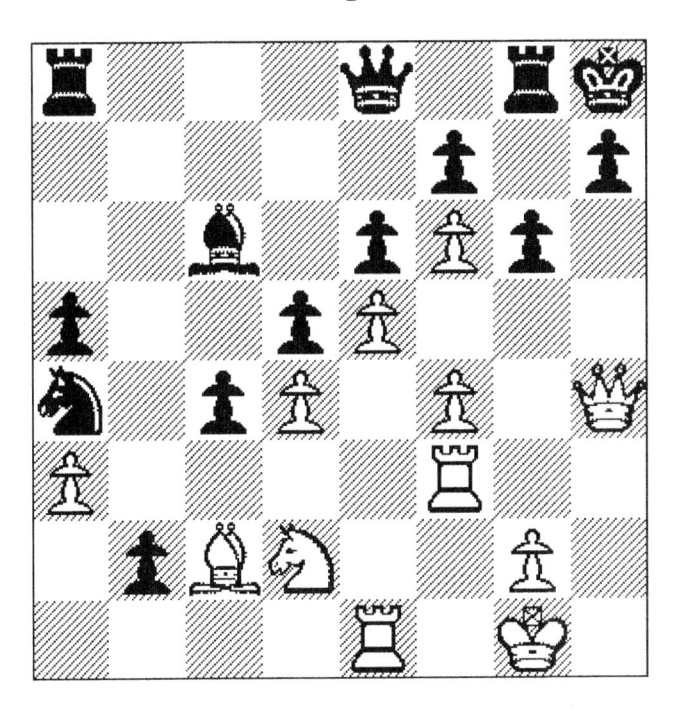

25. Rae1 Rg8 26. Rf3

The b1 square is safely guarded.
Black has no choice. Qf8(otherwise Qh7 Kh7 Rh3 mate) Rh3 h5 Qh5, with mate to follow.

Rg7 27. fg7

1-0

Game 21
The Berlin KID

December 29th 2013
White: Stockfish DD
Black: Lyudmil Tsvetkov
C65 Ruy Lopez, Berlin Defence

1. e4 e5 2. Nf3 Nc6 3. Bb5 Nf6 4. d3

As said, the Berlin Defence is usually a good way to try to get a favourable closed structure against Stockfish.

White chooses a quiet variation.

d6 5. d4

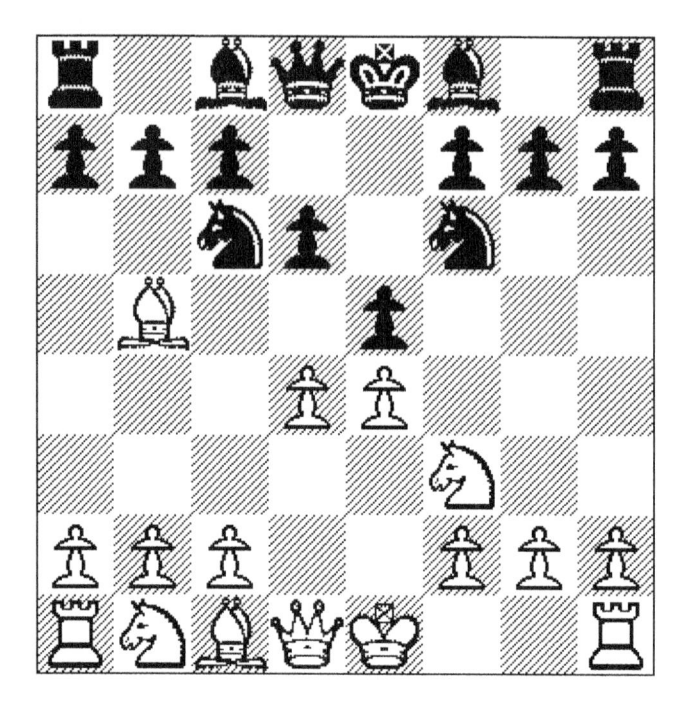

Well, this one is a surprise, moving the pawn to d4 at 2 separate pushes.

The engine threatens d4-d5.

Bd7 6. Nc3 Be7 7. d5 Nb8

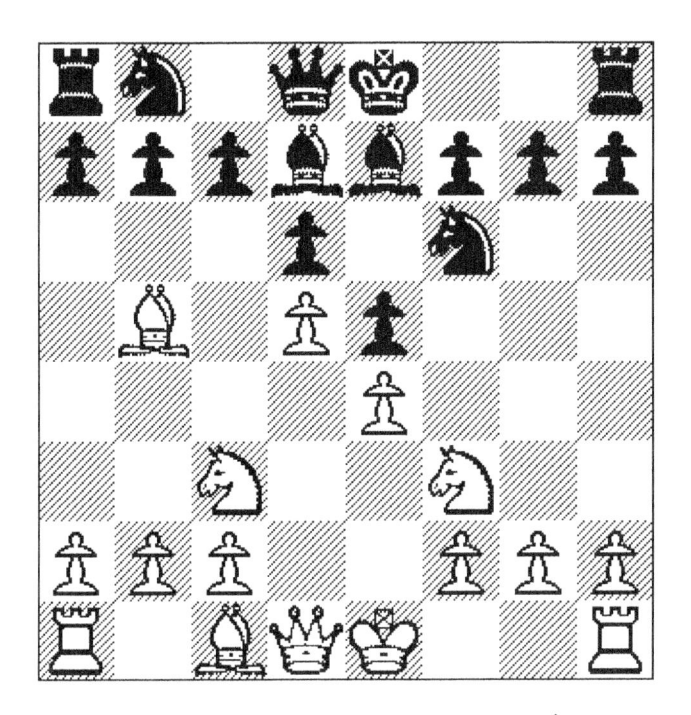

Bd7 Nbd7 unnecessarily develops the black knight, so Stockfish retreats its bishop.

8. Bc4 O-O 9. Qe2 Ne8 10. O-O Kh8

Black wants to push f5, but doing it straight is bad, as white has Ne5! de5 d6 check, subsequently picking the e7 bishop and opening the game. Therefore, the king leaves the a2-g8 diagonal.

11. Be3

Stockfish develops.

Rg8

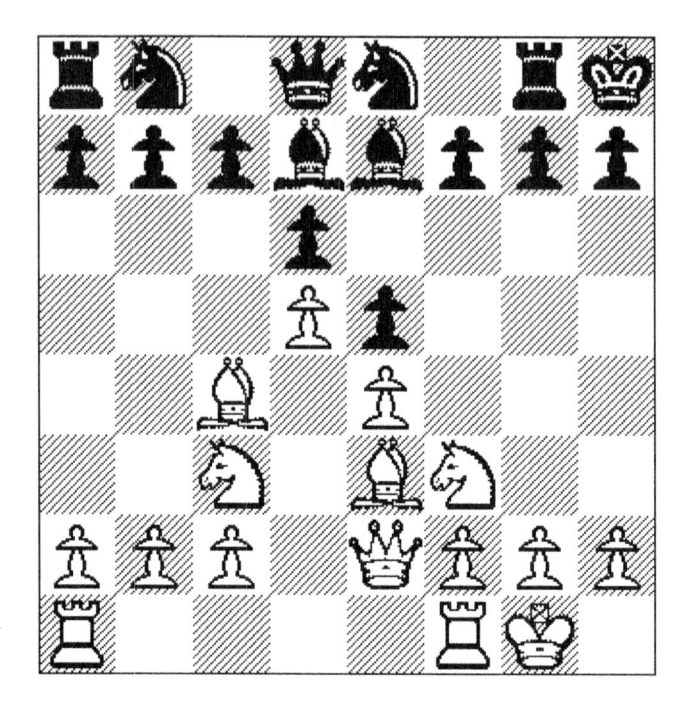

To some, this might seem like a strange move(the rook gets away from the f file it intends to open after f7-f5), but it has a logic attached to it. Black wants to play g6, to support the f5 pawn, but on that the opponent has Bh6, attacking the rook and gaining tempo.

11...f5 straight is again a mistake, this time a positional one, as after ef5 Bf5 h3(to prevent Bg4 pin), followed by Bd3 and Nd2-e4, white gets quite some edge with excellently placed central pieces and much better dark-square bishop.

12. b4

Stockfish initiates an outright assault on the queen side.

g6

Proceeding according to plan.

13. Rab1

The rook on b1 is more active than on a1, but apart from that, this move seemingly lacks purpose.

Nd2 was the much better choice, to follow up with f4, attempting to make use of its better development. Seemingly, in that case f5 f4 is insufficient, so black must continue with 13...g5!(stopping f4), followed by Rg6, Ng7, etc., with very complicated and unusual play.

f5

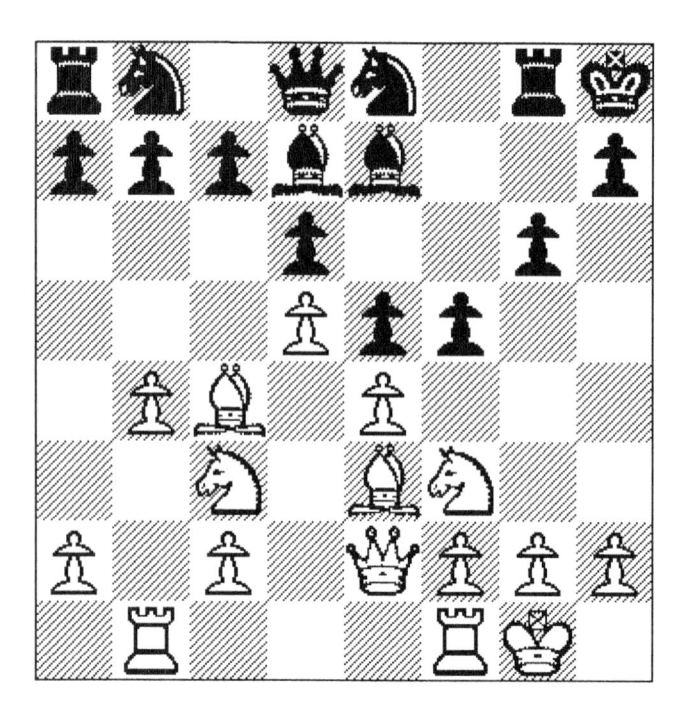

Now, already black enjoys decisive advantage. f5-f4 threatens.

14. Bd2

The bishops retreats. Who likes being kicked?
14. ef5 gf5 is not a tad better, while 14. g3 weakens too much the king shelter and black has different tactical shots, involving f4 and Bg4(maybe not immediately, only after playing Ng7-h5, etc.)

f4

A longer chain is one of the strongest positional assets in chess.

15. h3 g5 16. Nh2

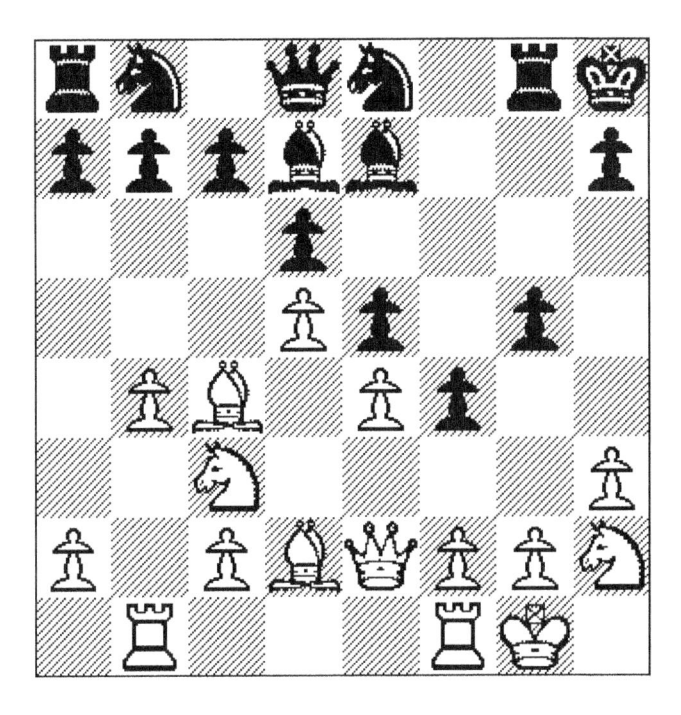

As if the g5-g4 threat has been stopped, and the queen controls the h5 square so the h7 pawn can not go there to support the storm, but black gradually brings in the reserve.

Nf6

Attacking the g4 square once more and supporting h5.

17. Ng4

Otherwise, black plays h5 and g4.

Bg4!

17...h5? 18. Nf6 Bf6 19. Qh5 check is simply a blunder, while in the present position the knight is more valuable than the bishop.

18. hg4 h5!

Temporarily sacrificing a pawn.
White should capture. 19. f3 hg4 20. fg4 Qc8, with subsequent Ng4 is no option.

19. gh5 g4 20. h6 Qe8

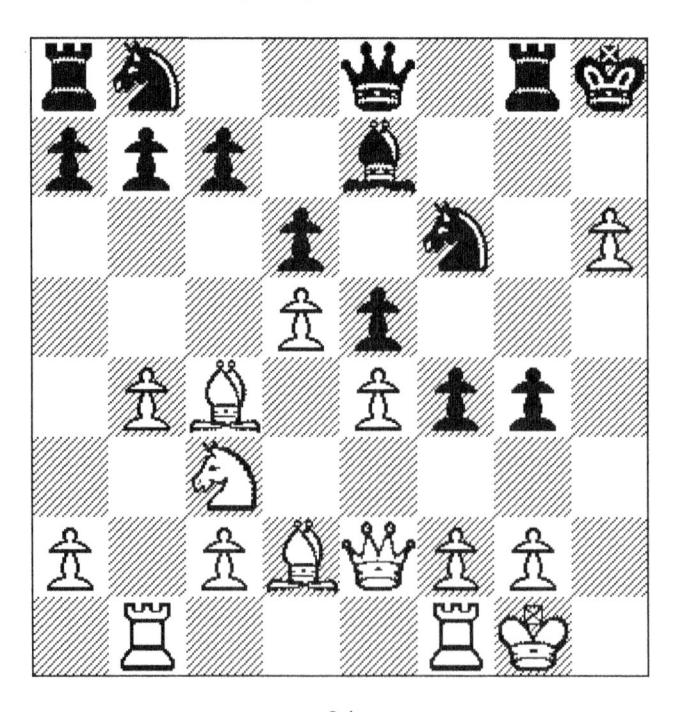

Once the queen reaches h5, the game is more or less decided.

Nb5 is never a threat at that, as black has Na6, defending c7.

21. g3

Qh5, followed by Rg6-h6 and mate, has been the threat. Now, after black answers with f3, the h6 pawn is at least defended by the bishop on d2, so the black rook can not capture it.

f3 22. Qd3 Qh5

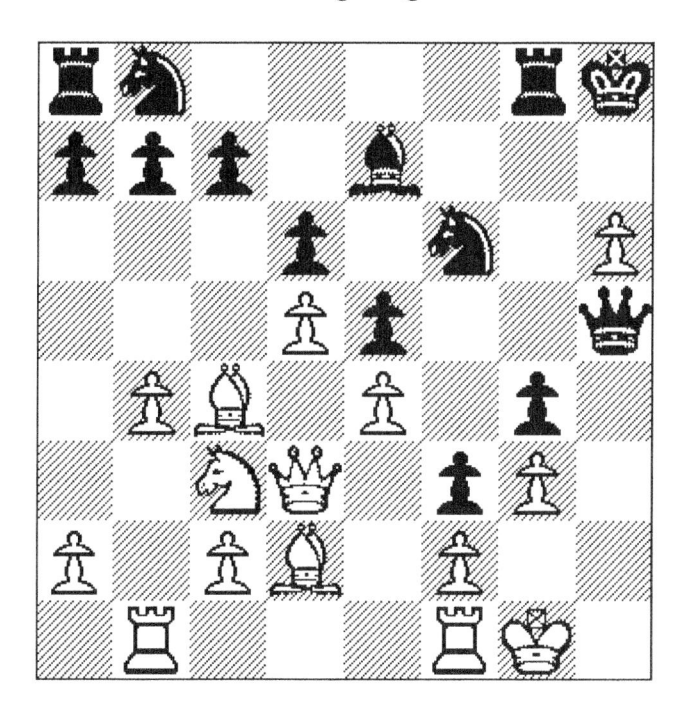

Black threatens Qh3-g2 mate.

23. Rfe1

The rook evacuates the f1 square. Now, on 23...Qh3, white has 24. Qf1, defending g2.

Rg6

Attacking the pawn and threatening to seal the game after Bf8-h6, with subsequent transfer of the rook to the h file.

24. Nb5

The c7 square is weak.

Bd8

There are thousand ways to win, Na6, Nd7, possibly even Bf8, but that should be sufficient too, though obviously not optimal and the product of time trouble or something else.

25. a4 a6

Shoo, shoo, knight.

26. Na3 Nh7

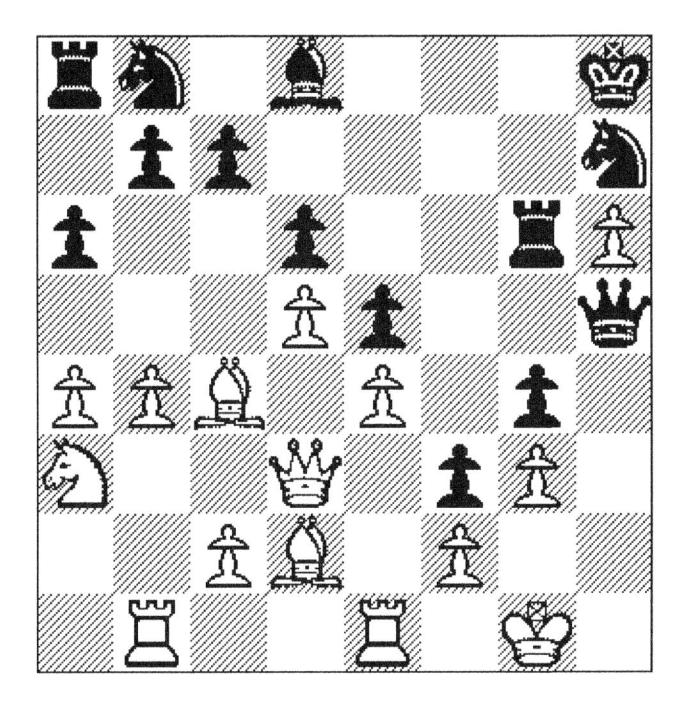

With the aim to cover the g5 square with either the bishop or knight, with subsequent rook capture on h6 and mate on h1.

27. Bb5

Stockfish is in a sacrificial mood. Obviously, it sees threats when they are closer, but not in much longer lines.

ab5

Ng5 also wins.

28. Nb5 Ng5 29. Nd6

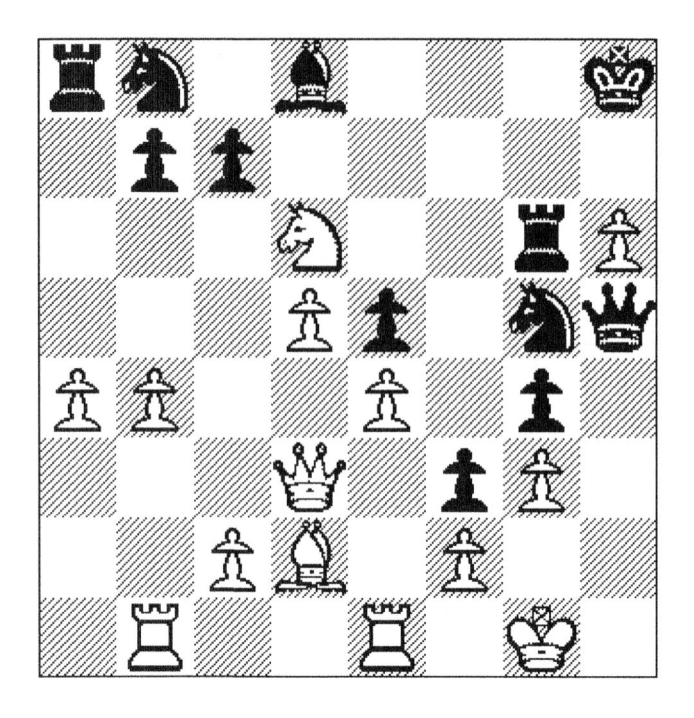

This is already too much. Instead of resigning, the engine continues gobbling up pawns.

cd6 30. Bg5 Bg5 31. Qc4

Qc8 threatens. Why not a perpetual?

Na6 32. Qf1 Rh6

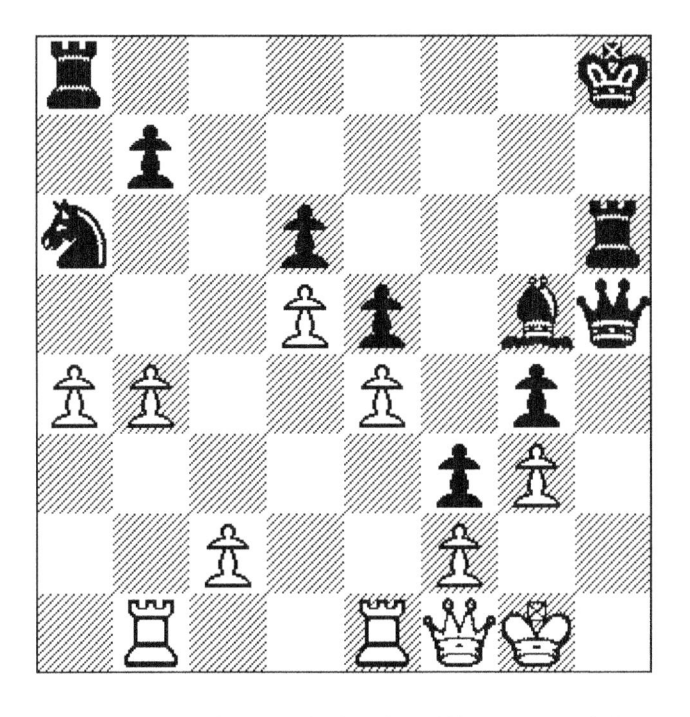

Well, that is it. Stockfish is still resourceful.

**33. Qg2 fg2 34. Kg2 Qh3
35. Kg1 Qh1 mate**

Game 22
Dancing knights

December 31st 2013
White: Lyudmil Tsvetkov
Black: Stockfish DD
D00 Queen's Pawn Game

**1. f4 Nf6 2. Nf3 d5 3. d4 e6 4. e3 c5
5. c3 Nc6 6. Bd3 c4**

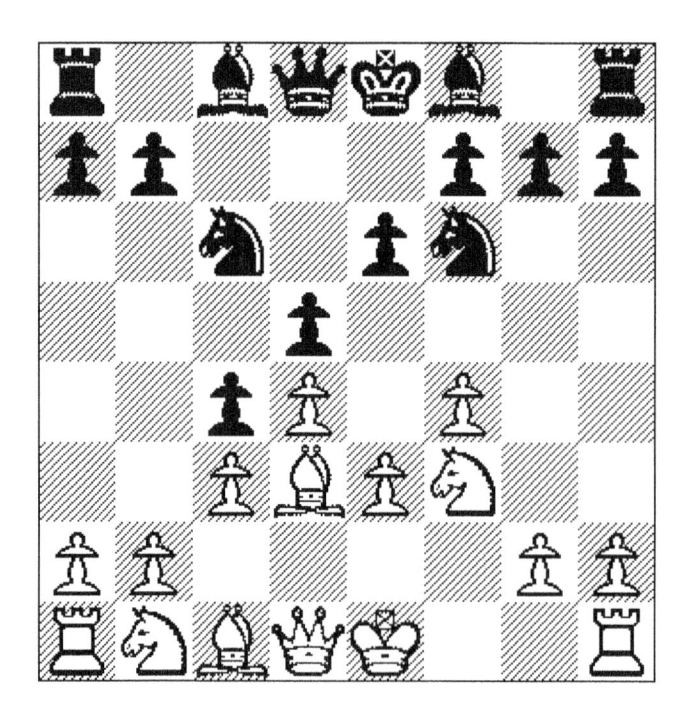

This is an already familiar pattern, but Stockfish chooses to close the game even further with c4.

7. Bc2 b5 8. a3 Bd6 9. O-O Bb7 10. Ne5

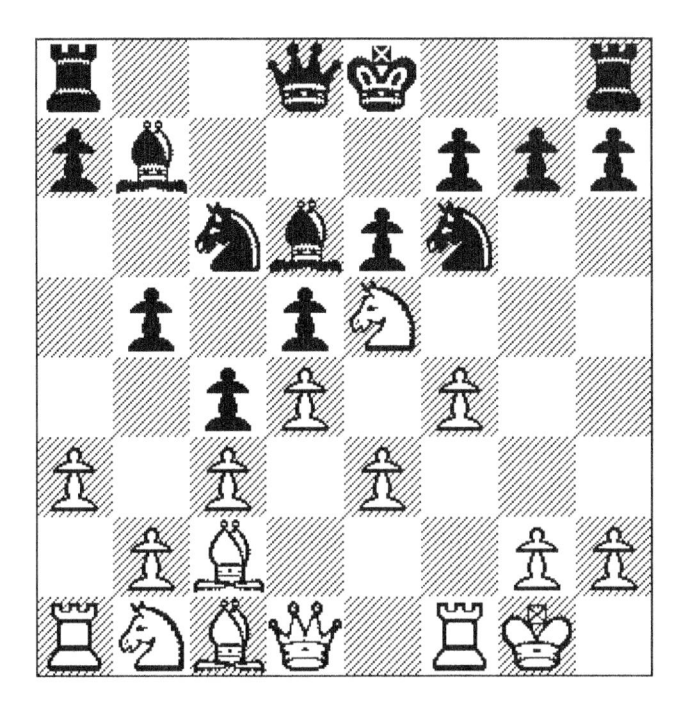

After the pawn wall is built, white starts finding more active places for its pieces.

O-O

Stockfish should have jumped to e4 now, with fairly equal position.

11. Nd2

Now, the knight hop is already impossible, as the d2 knight has taken control of e4.
Similar small hiccups frequently decide games.

Qc7 12. Qf3

The queen attacks e4 once more.

Rad8

Centralisation could not be bad.

13. g4

Having the center under control, white initiates an immediate pawn storm.

g6 14. g5

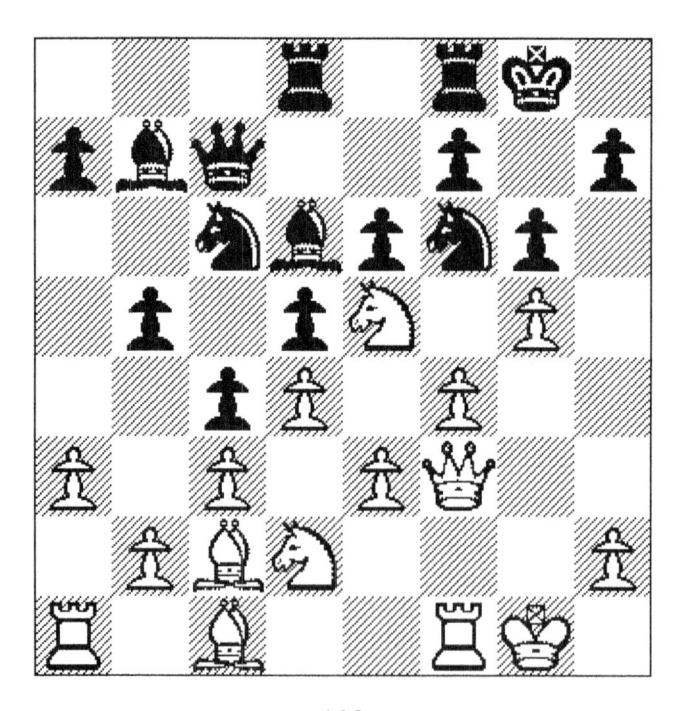

Where should the black knight retreat now?

Seemingly, Nh5 and Ne8 are more or less equal, as from both squares the knight can reach g7, though on h5 the knight also blocks the h file.

Nh5 15. Qg4

Clearing the f3 square for the rook to transfer to the h file.

a5 16. Rf3 Ne7

Heading for f5.

The black knights seem to have quite enjoyable outpost squares.

17. Rh3 Nf5

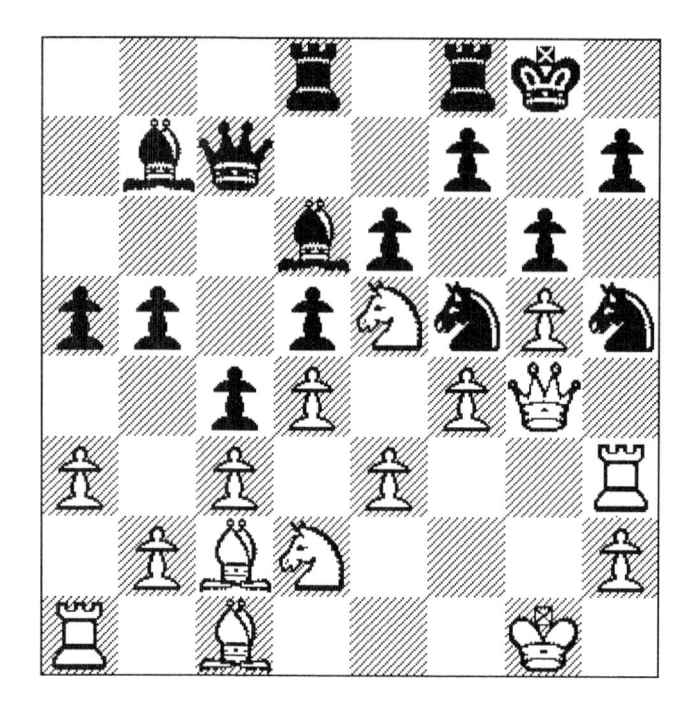

Funny position, is not it?

White enjoys quite some space advantage, though black seems to adequately defend everything.

Rh5 gh5 Qh5 does not work now, as the f5 knight successfully covers the b1-h7 diagonal.

If necessary, black can also play Nfg7, to additionally protect its counterpart on h5 and avoid any pawn structure compromisation. White has no option but to continue with development.

18. Ndf3 Nfg7

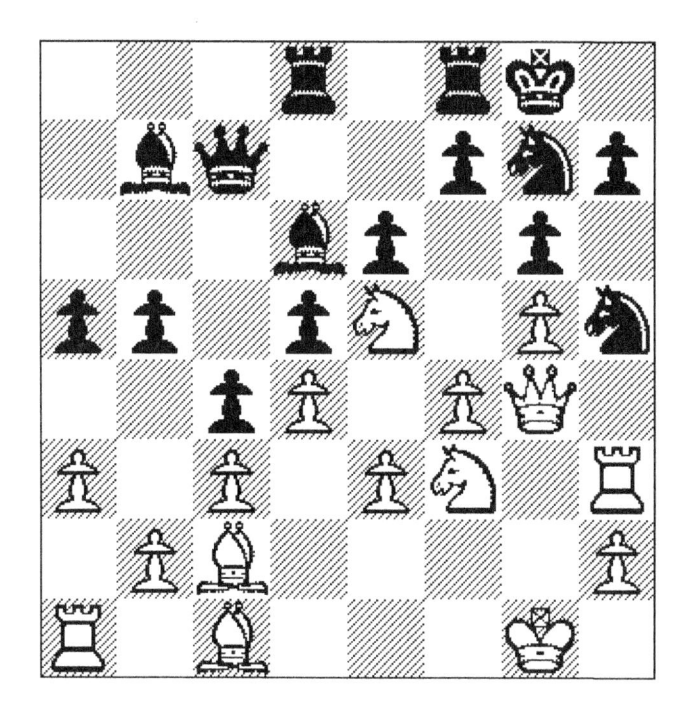

I am posting this again: very funny position, is not it?

19. Bd2 Ra8 20. Qg2

No obvious attacking continuations in sight, so the queen frees the g4 square, intending to transfer there the knight from e5, to target the f6 and h6 squares, while its counterpart on f3 to e5.

b4

Stockfish starts a counterattack.

21. Ng4

Indeed.

Capturing on b4 completely makes no sense, as this will open the game much to the chagrin of white.

Kh8

No checks, from either h6 or f6.

22. Nfe5

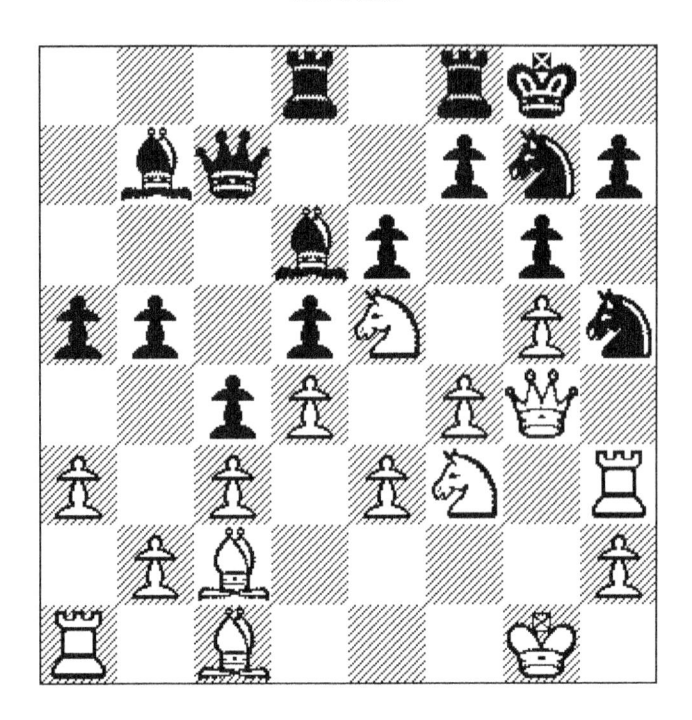

Plan executed.

b3?

This move gains much space on the queen side, but fully closes the game there, so from now on Stockfish will be devoid of any realistic counterplay.

Of course, one can not expect from Stockfish to see such deep positional moves.

22...ba3, followed by Rb8, might have been preferable, though after ba3 and Bc1, the white light-square bishop successfully defends both the a3 pawn, as well as the b2 penetration point.

23. Bd1

Bb1 shuts out the rook on a1 for eternity.

Rac8 24. Nf6

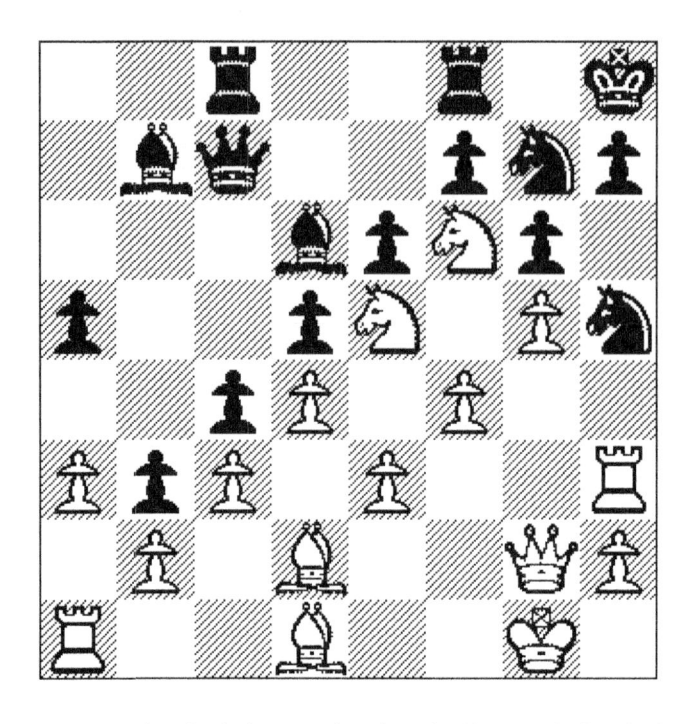

Now, the knight on h5 is challenged, both by the knight on f6 and the bishop on d1. White starts getting the upper hand.

Rg8

Stockfish finds nothing better than to sac the exchange.

White threatens to capture twice on h5, with a rout. 24...Nf6 is no option, as after 25. gf6 Nf5(Ne8 Qg5 Qd8(attacking again f6) Ng4) 26. Bg4(with the aim to destroy the precious f5 defender) Rg8 27. Kh1(to evacuate the g file and make possible Bf5) Qd8 28. Bf5 gf5 29. Rh7, black gets mated.

25. Nfg4

There are different ways to win, but I, probably under time pressure, go for the safest way, developing more pieces while risking nothing.

Of course, capturing on g8 makes no sense.

Rgf8

Stockfish shuffles around.

26. Be2 Nf5 27. Kh1 Be7 28. Rg1

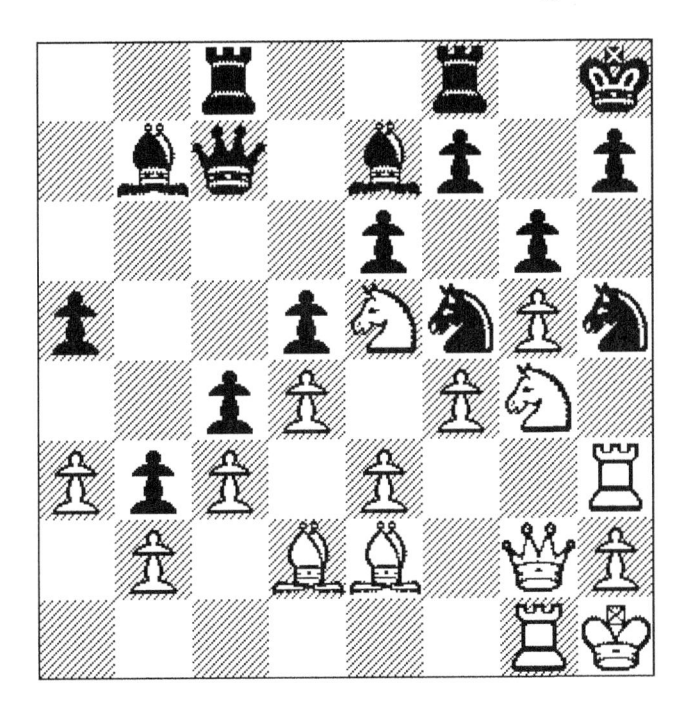

White is ready for the final assault.

Nfg7 29. Nh6

Let's check if h6 or f6 is a cozier location. f7 is under attack.

Bd6 30. Rh4

Freeing the h3 square for the queen.

Qe7

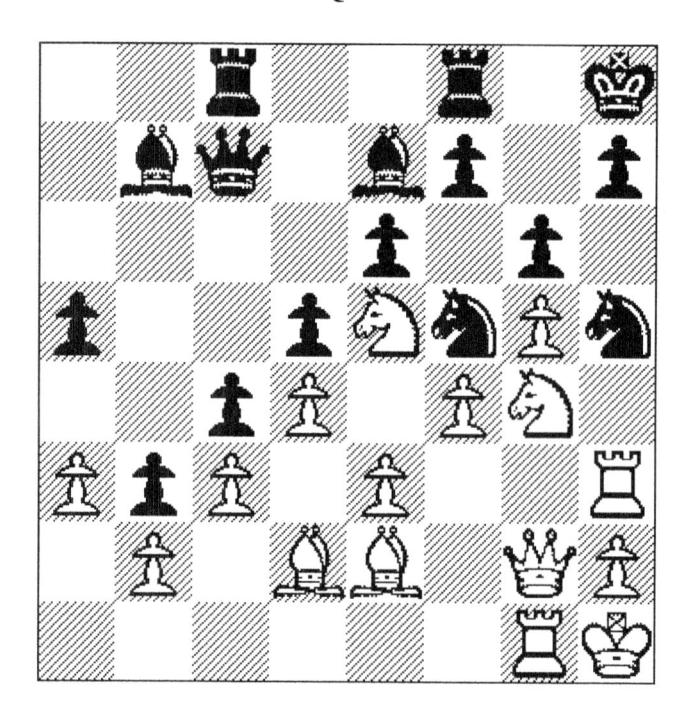

30...f6 is impossible, as after 31. gf6 Rf6 32. Bh5 gh5 33. Rh5, black can not capture on h5 with the knight, as Qg8 mates.

31. Qh3 Rc7 32. Nhg4

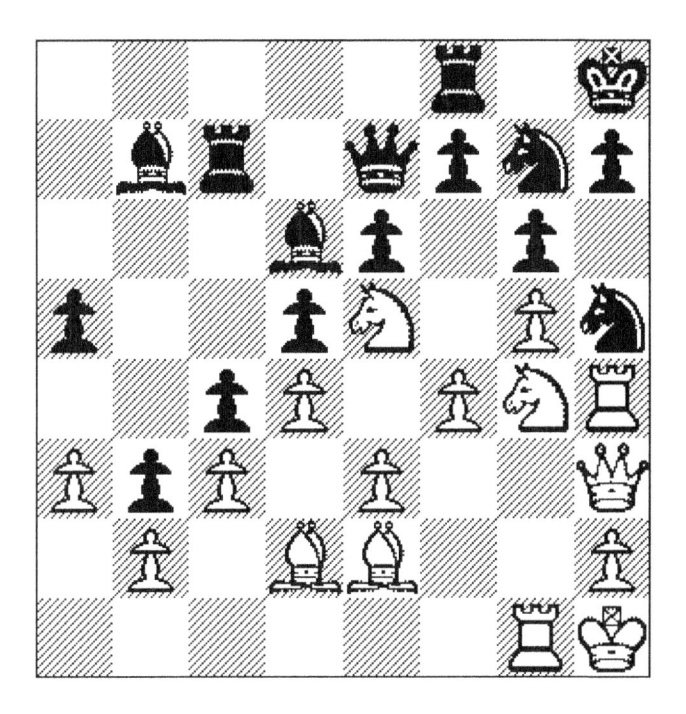

A final dislocation to f6 should already decide the game.

The white knight dance has paid off in the end.

Please note, that at this point into the game, not a single pawn or piece for either side has been captured, but black is completely lost.

After Nf6 is played, the h7 square is impossible to defend, too many white pieces attack it.

Be5

Getting rid of at least a single attacker, but that solves nothing.

33. fe5 Rg8

33...Qg5 loses to 34. Nf6 Qh6(no other escape squares) 35. Bh5 Nh5 36. Nh5 gh5 37. Rh5

34. Nf6

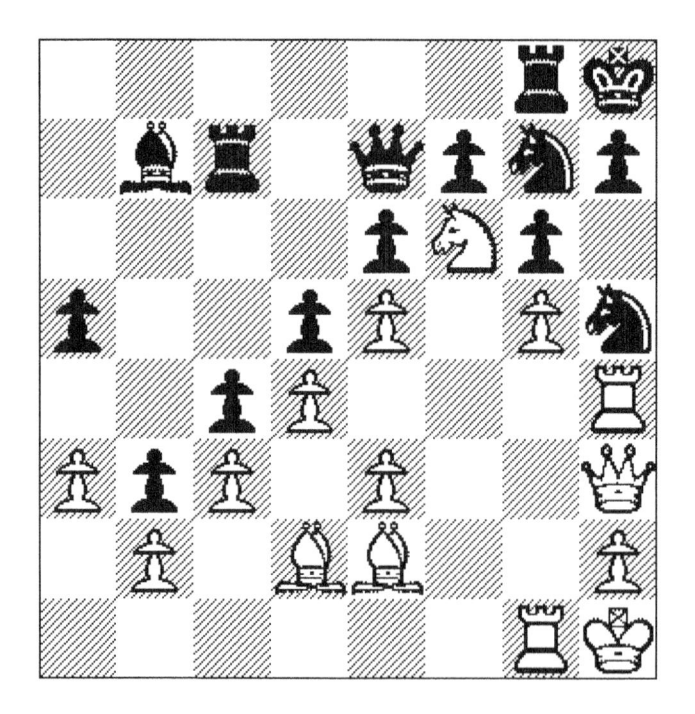

One more shot at this. The white position is so overwhelming.

Qd8 35. Rg3

Preparing Kg1(so that the black knight does not take on g3 with check), Qf1, Rh3, Qd1, and the h5 point finally crumbles.

Nf5

Stockfish would not like to wait more.

36. Bh5 Nh4

Ng3 is identical.

37. Qh4

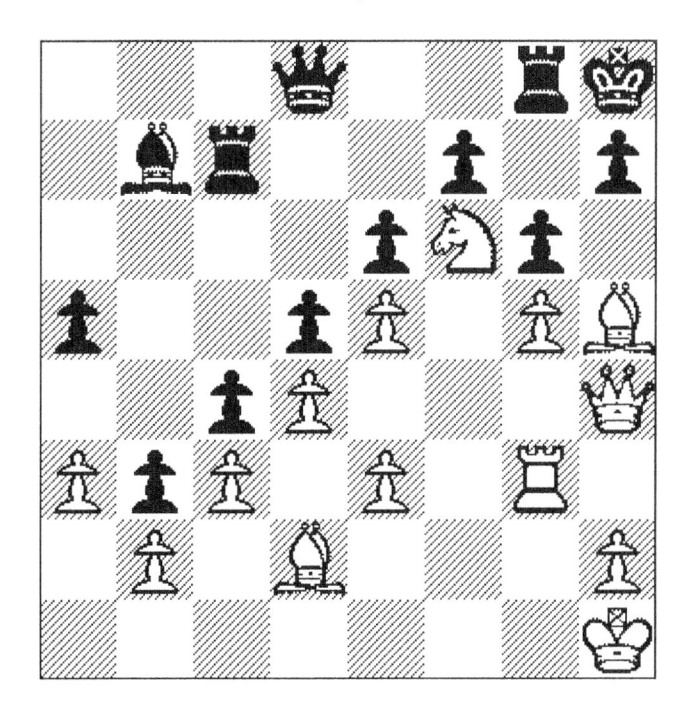

Stockfish resigned.

After 37...gh5 38. Qh5 Rg7 39. Rh3, the only way for black to prevent mate on h7 is to sac the queen on g8.

Game 23
New paradigm

January 9th 2014
White: Lyudmil Tsvetkov
Black: Stockfish DD
C20 King's Pawn Game

1. c4

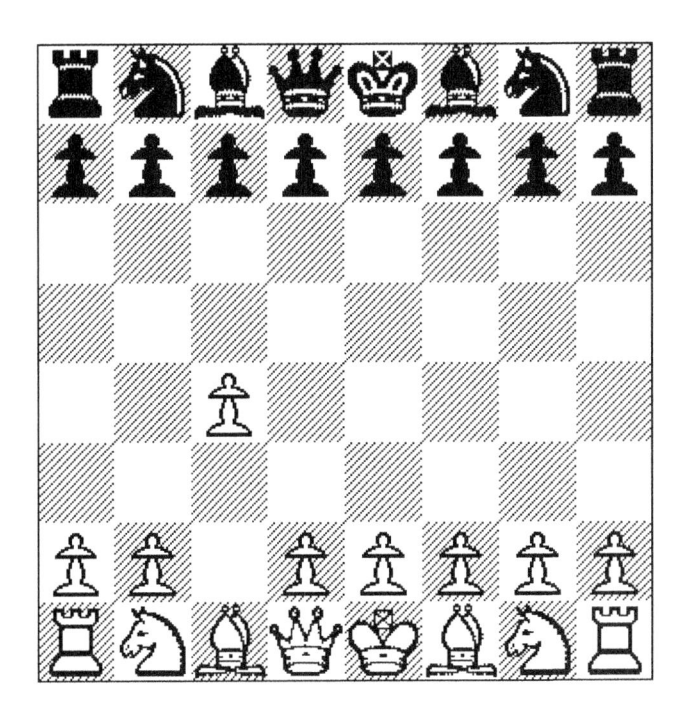

An excellent move, actually, the best possible first move, but that will need a lot of time to prove scientifically. The ease with which Stockfish is crushed in this game might be just a hint.

e5 2. d3

Nc3 is definitely better, as black could have pushed d5 now, but I am just starting to employ this system.

Nf6 3. e4!

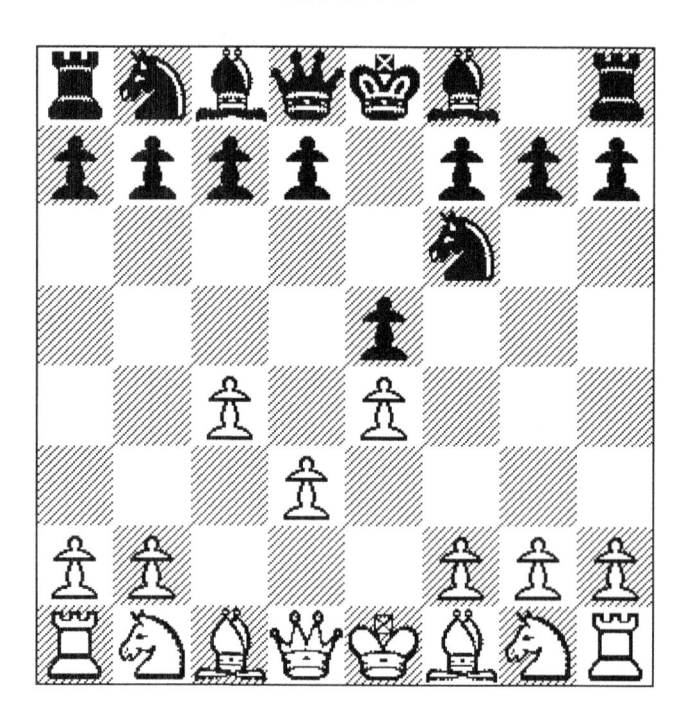

Strange as it might seem, this is the best move.

White is binding the central d5 square, so that, if black can not push d7-d5, it will lack any substantial counterplay.

Bc5

Developing and attacking the f2 point.

4. Be2

It is not necessary to test a possible Nf3 Ng4 d4. The bishop takes the g4 square under control.

d6 5. Nf3 O-O 6. O-O Nc6 7. Nc3 Nd4

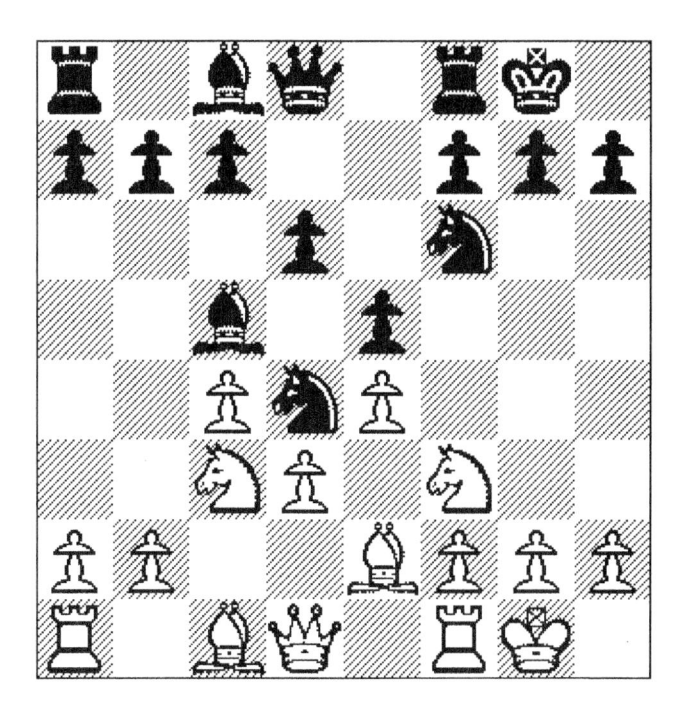

Black has developed and already places a central knight outpost on d4. White has the advantage, though, because of the central bind upon the d5 square, as well as the opportunity to push an early f2-f4.

8. Nd4

Capturing the knight and freeing the way for the f pawn.

Bd4 9. Kh1

Before pushing f4, white should unpin the pawn.
9. Be3 is stupid, of course, that might double the white pawns, but black has even better with c6 and Qb6.

c6

The d5 square is taken control of, and d5 and b5 potential thrusts prepared.

10. f4

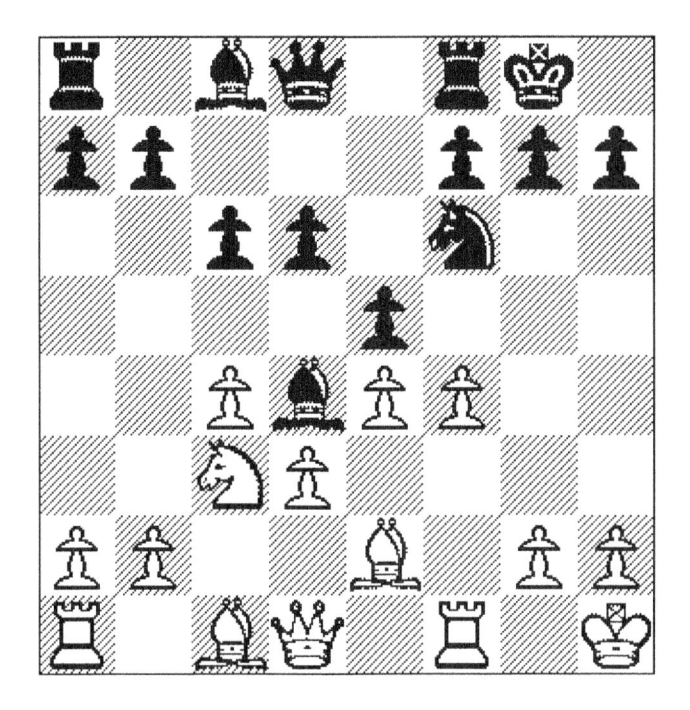

Let's take stock of this position.

White is definitely better. It has already started a pawn storm with f4, while the black d4 bishop, although seemingly very active, in reality attacks nothing.

Different things already threaten, like fe5 de5(Be5 d4) Bg5, pinning the knight, or even, under the appropriate circumstances, f5, followed by g4-g5.

10...g6 is an outright blunder, because of 11. fe5 de5 12. Bg5, winning the knight.

h6

Stockfish senses the danger and makes the bishop pin from g5 impossible.

10...Qb6(aiming to trade dark-square bishops on e3) might have been a bit better, but after 11. Bf3 Be3(ef4 Na4 and Bf4) 12. g3!, white retains quite some edge due to its considerably stronger central pawn structure.

10...Bc3 is no option, of course, as this cedes the pair of bishops, and in a more open position the bishop pair is much more valuable than existing pawn weaknesses.

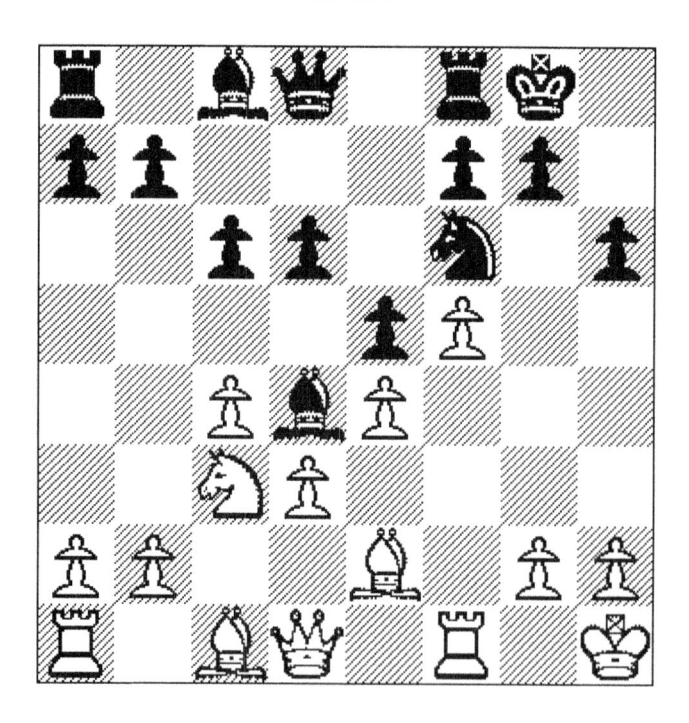

11. f5!

Bf3 was an alternative, but this one is stronger.

Now, white threatens to immediately pawn-storm with g2-g4.

On 11...d5, white has 12. g4! de4(dc4 is equivalent) 13. g5!, sacrificing a pawn with tremendous initiative. Whether black could save that with perfect play is anyone's guess, but white has good winning chances.

11...Qb6 is met by Na4(otherwise black trades bishops on e3, while keeping sentinel of the g5 square), followed by g4.

11...Nh7 is not good either, as after g4 Qh4 Bd2 and Be1, the queen gets driven away.

Bd7

Stockfish decides to go it slowly.

12. g4

The faster, the better.

g5, as well as h4 Nh7 Qe1(defending the h4 pawn), followed by Qg3 and g5, threaten.

b5

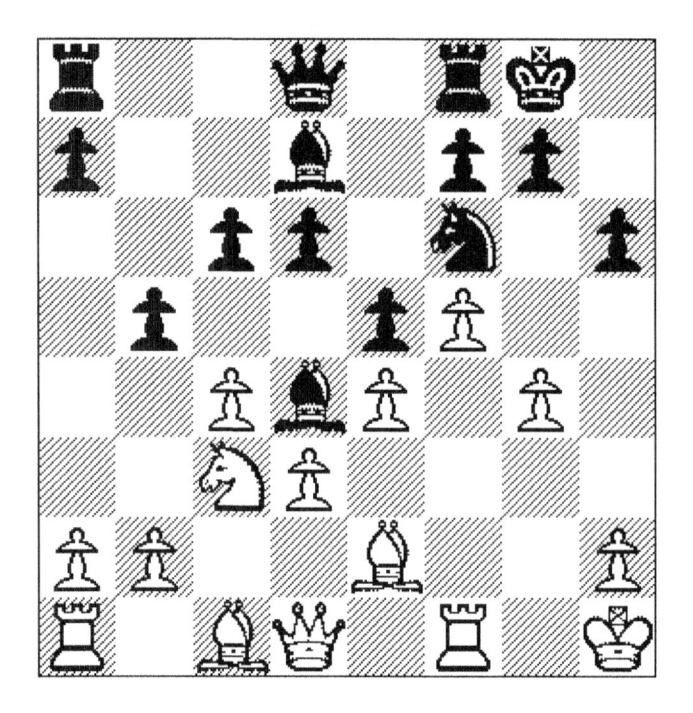

The engine counterattacks, but is seemingly much slower.

As said, on 12...Nh7, 13. Qe1, followed by Qg3 and h4, ensure white an almost-winning position.

13. g5!

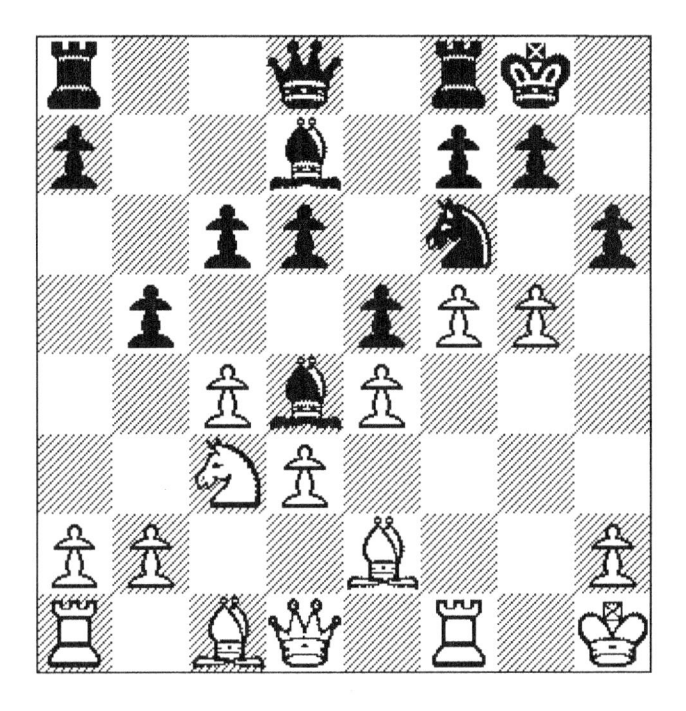

Of course. Only thing white has in mind is a tempestuous attack.

hg5

13...Nh7 14. gh6 is hardly an option.

14. Bg5 b4

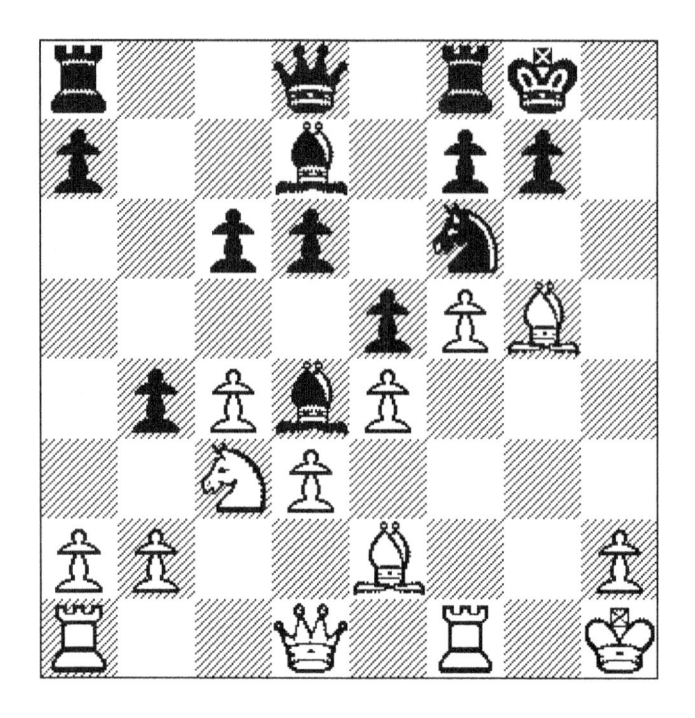

14...bc4 is too slow, white simply plays Qe1-h4, Rf3-h3, with a bust.

On 14...Qb6, white still has 15. Qe1 Nh7(Be3 Qg3 Bg5 Qg5, followed by Rg1, with large-looming threats) 16. Be7(or Qh4) Re8 17. f6, and black is lost.

Stockfish decides to win tempo by kicking the knight.

15. Na4

15. Qe1 bc3 16. Qh4(or even bc3) cb2 17. Rb1, followed by Rf3, might also have been winning, and in a more spectacular fashion, but I decide on a more careful approach.

Qe7

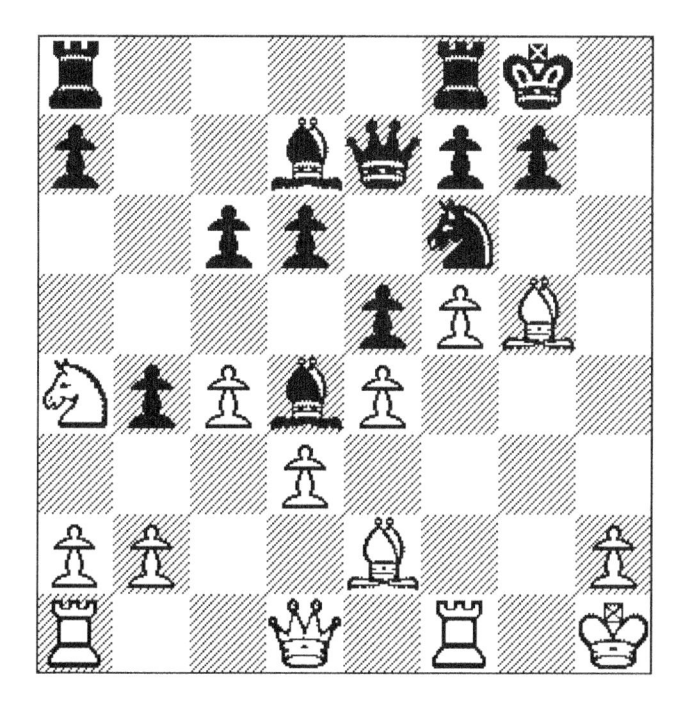

That pin is very nasty.

On 15...Qc7, white might search for quick mates after Bf6(not sure if available in all lines, not quite having checked it), but has also a safer and much more powerful way to seal the game with 16. Qe1 Nh7 17. Qh4, and black is busted.

15...Kh7(to bring the rook to h8 and then play Kg8) more or less leads to the same after 16. Rf3 Rh8 17. Rh3 Kg8 18. Rh8 Kh8 19. Qe1, followed by a tempo-gaining check on h4.

16. Qe1

Proceeding according to plan.

c5

Attacking the knight on a4. What else?

17. Qh4

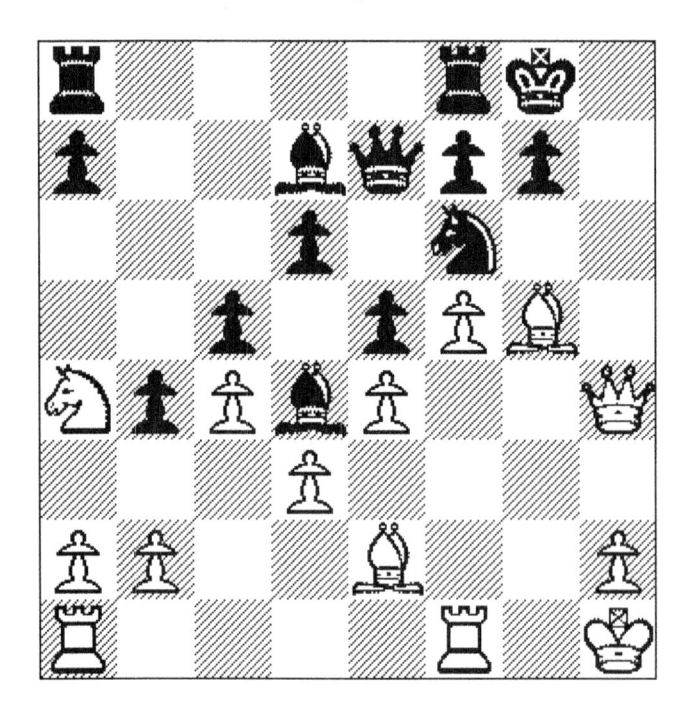

Well, that is a win in a couple of moves, white threatens the inevitable Rf3-h3, but I suddenly start playing in the weakest possible way.

Rfd8

At least to free the f8 square for the king, so there is no mate after Rf3 Kf8 Qh8 Ng8. Of course, the queen falls.

18. Rg1?

Thinking this is equivalent to Rf3, but black has surprising tactics to ward-off the most unpleasant threats.

Bf2!

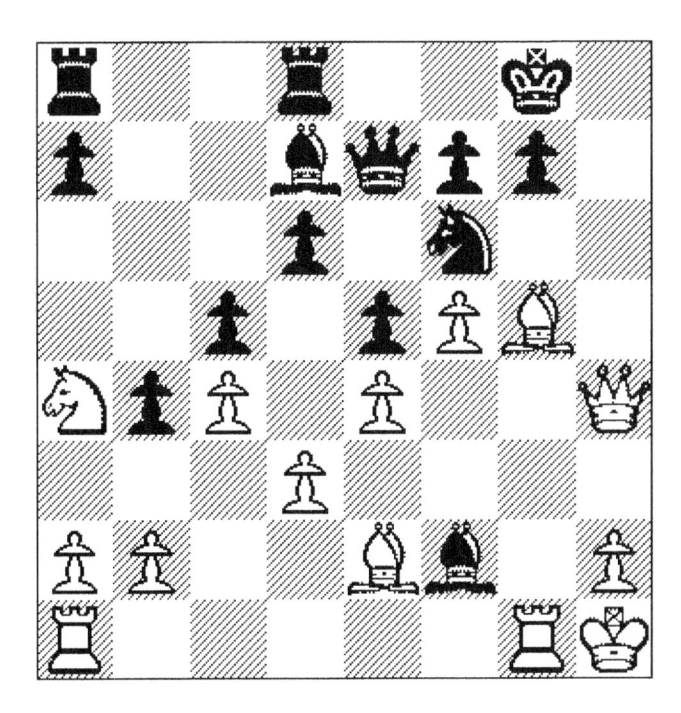

Well, this is one I simply can not see.
Engines excel in similar moves.
In distinction to a rook on f3, the rook on g1 does not guard the f2 square. In the former case, Rf2 has been

deciding on the spot. Now, Stockfish manages to successfully regroup and as a result white wins only a piece.

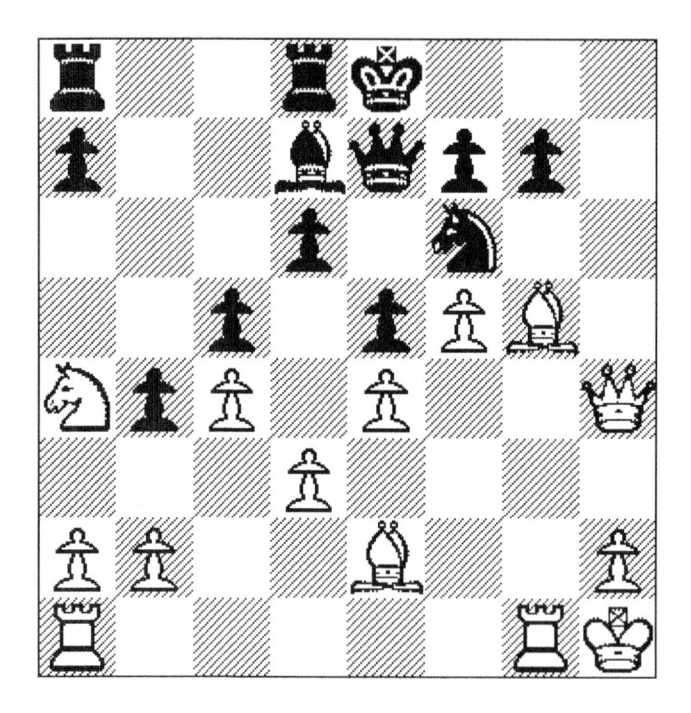

19. Qf2 Kf8 20. Qh4 Ke8

Well, that is all the distinction. Stockfish has gained a valuable tempo by sacrificing its bishop, the king has escaped to e8, and now the white queen check on h8 does not win the queen after Ng8, as Stockfish can interpose its own queen on f8.

21. Bf6

I don't see anything better.

Qf6 22. Qf6 gf6

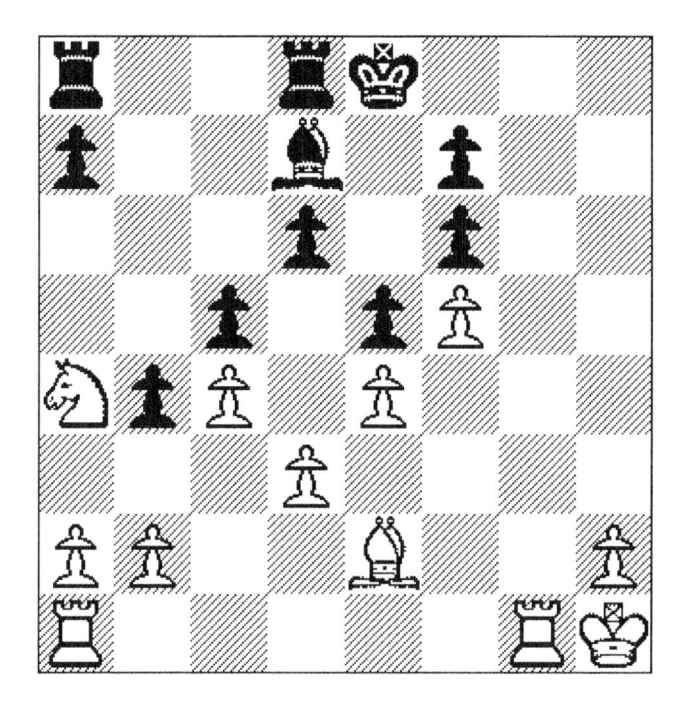

The dust has cleared. Full piece ahead plus an h passed pawn should be more than sufficient for an easy win.

23. Rg8

Changing rooks. It actually does not matter very much how white continues.

Ke7 24. Rd8 Kd8 25. b3

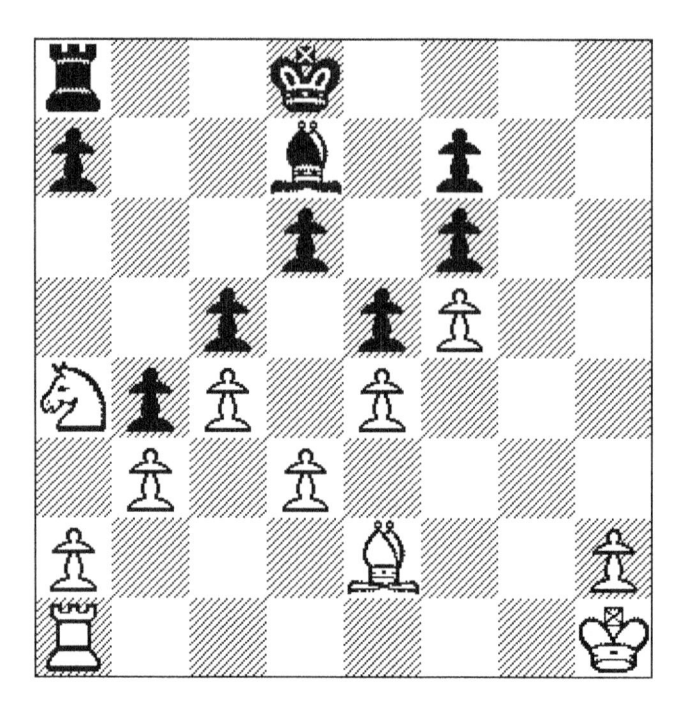

Defending the knight.

Ke7 26. Rg1 Bc6 27. h4

Full speed on the promotion path.
Interestingly, Stockfish still does not resign.

Rh8 28. Rg4 Rh5 29. Kh2

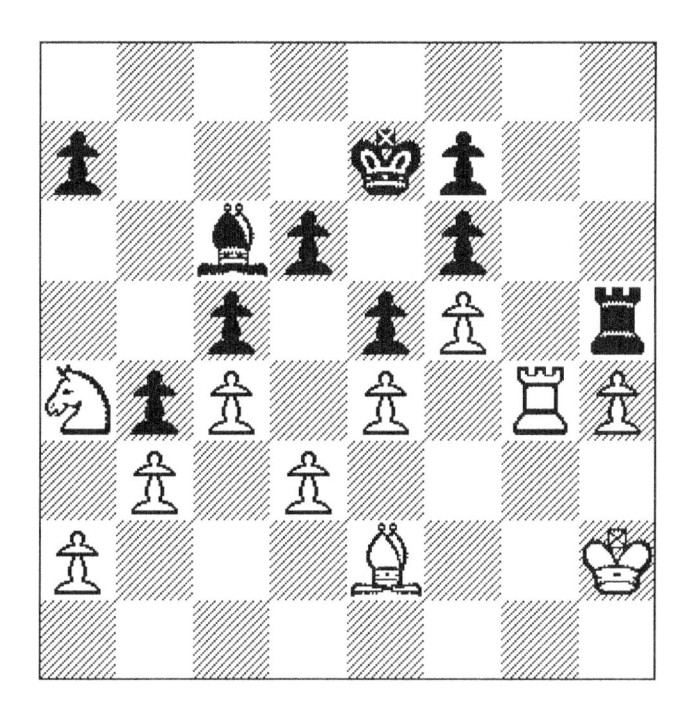

Once the king gets active, the advantage increases.

Ba4

Otherwise, the knight might hop to even better places via b2-d1-e3.

30. ba4 a5

The attempt to fully close the game is just an illusion. White is a full piece up, after all.

31. Kh3 Rh8 32. Rg2 Rb8 33. Bd1

Preventing b4-b3, with a whiff of a counterplay.

Rh8 34. h5 Ke8 35. Kh4 Ke7

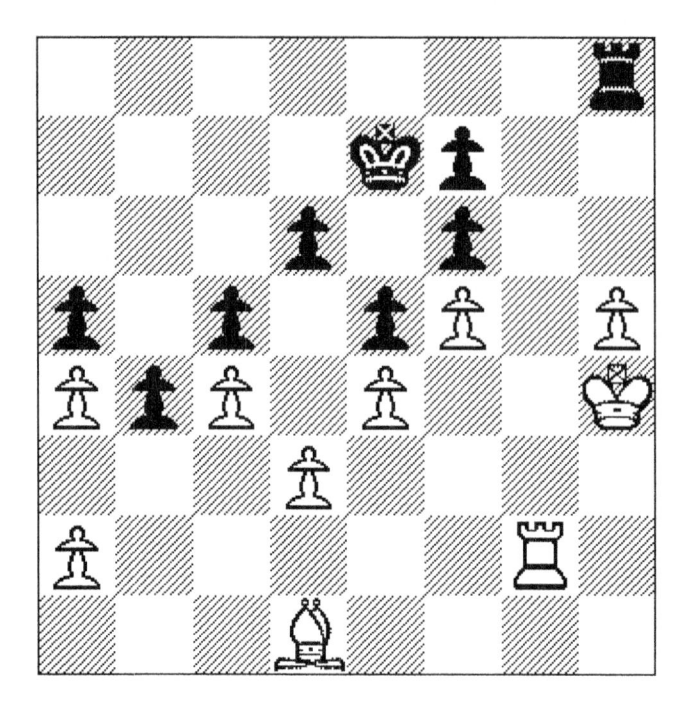

The white passer has advanced, but h5-h6 seems impossible to play.

White should break on the queen side.

36. Kg3

Stockfish resigned at last.

The white king travels to b3, after which a2-a3 is pushed.

In the case of ba3, the b file gets opened.

Otherwise, white plays ab4 ab4, getting a second passer on the a file.

If ab4 cb4 instead, white breaks with d4.
Resistance is meaningless.

Game 24
I have a crush on you

May 31st 2014
White: Lyudmil Tsvetkov
Black: Stockfish 5
D00 Queen's Pawn Game

**1. f4 d5 2. Nf3 Nf6 3. d4 c5
4. e3 Nc6 5. c3 e6 6. Bd3 c4
7. Bc2 Bd6 8. O-O b5 9. a3 Bb7
10. Nbd2 a5 11. Ne5**

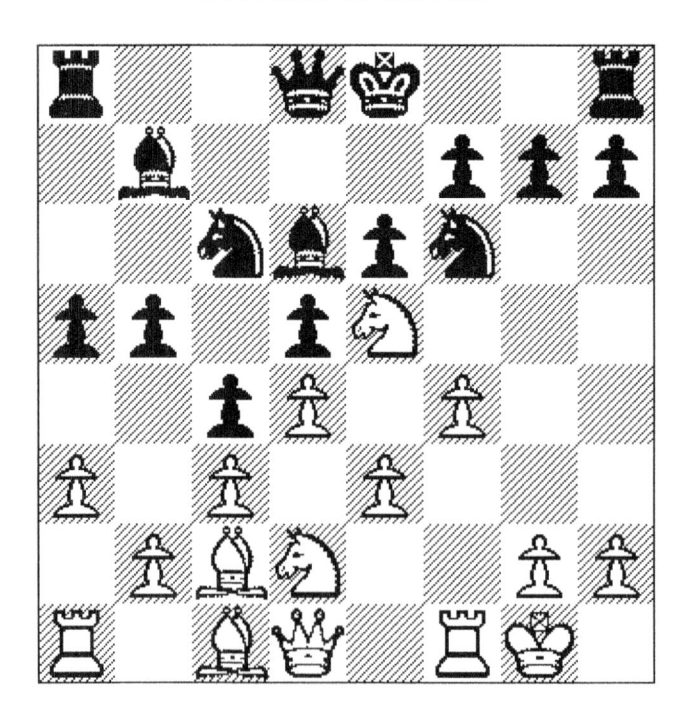

A familiar opening scheme. Stockfish has again pushed an early c4.

Qb6

Yielding pressure along the a7-g1 diagonal and supporting a b5-b4 push.

12. Qf3 O-O 13. g4 b4

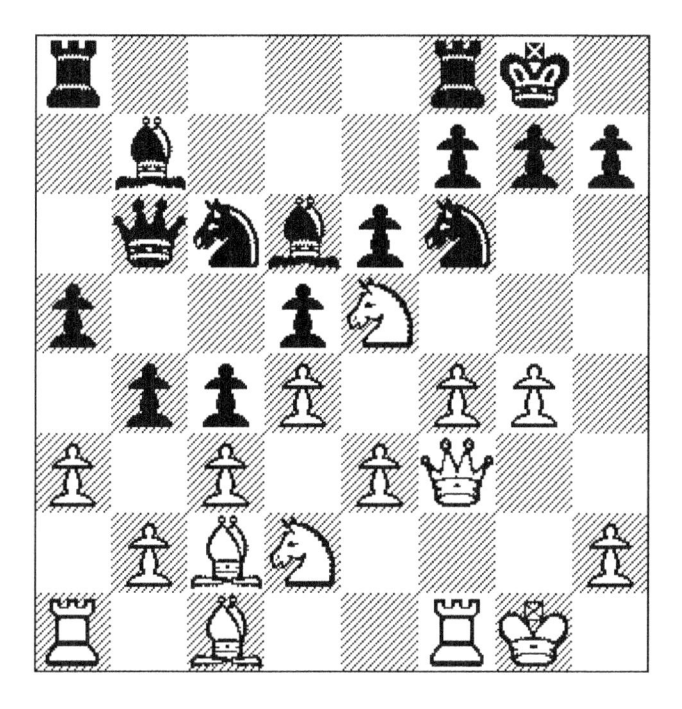

Who is faster now?

14. g5

Seemingly, white is much speedier.

The black knight can not retreat, as after 14...Ne8, white seals it with 15. Bh7! Kh7 16. Qh5 Kg8 17. Rf3 g6(f6 g6) 18. Qh6 Ng7 19. Rh3 Nh5(blocking the h file) 20. Ng4 Be7(otherwise Nf6 and Qh8 mate) 21. Rh5! gh5 22. Nf6 Bf6 23. gf6, with mate on g7 to follow.

b3

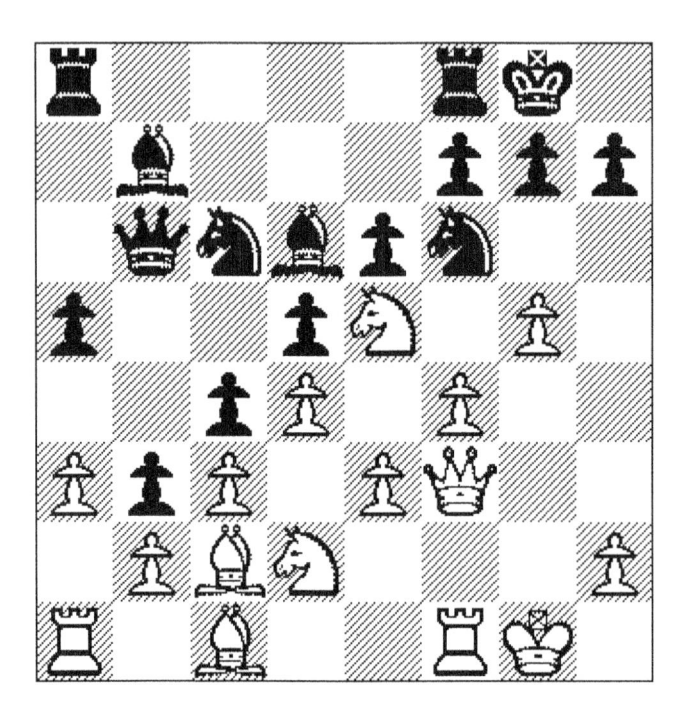

The engine is counterattacking to at least muddle things up.

15. gf6

Going the most straightforward way.

bc2

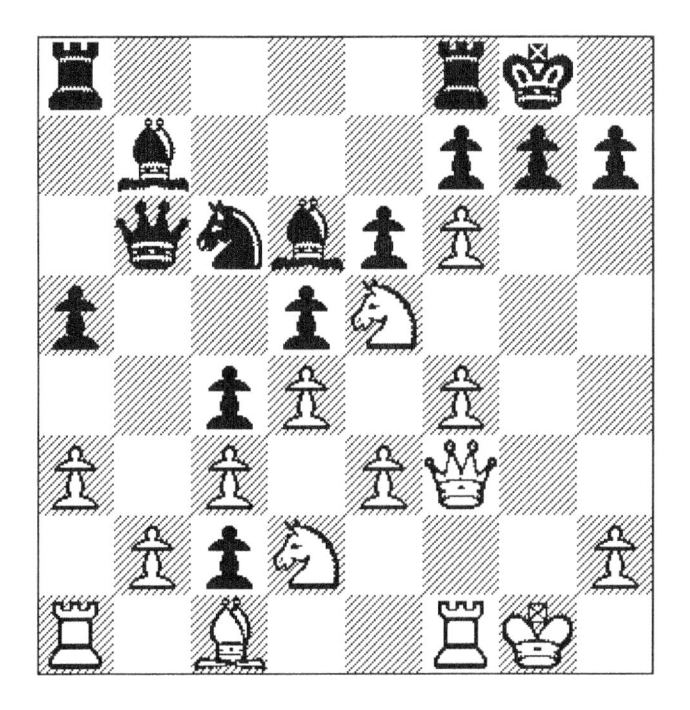

Anytime soon, Stockfish will promote a queen on c1.

16. Qg4

Mate on g7 threatens.

g6 17. Rf3

The rook lift should quickly decide.

Rfb8

Freeing the f8 square for the black bishop. 17...Kh8 does not help either.

18. Rh3

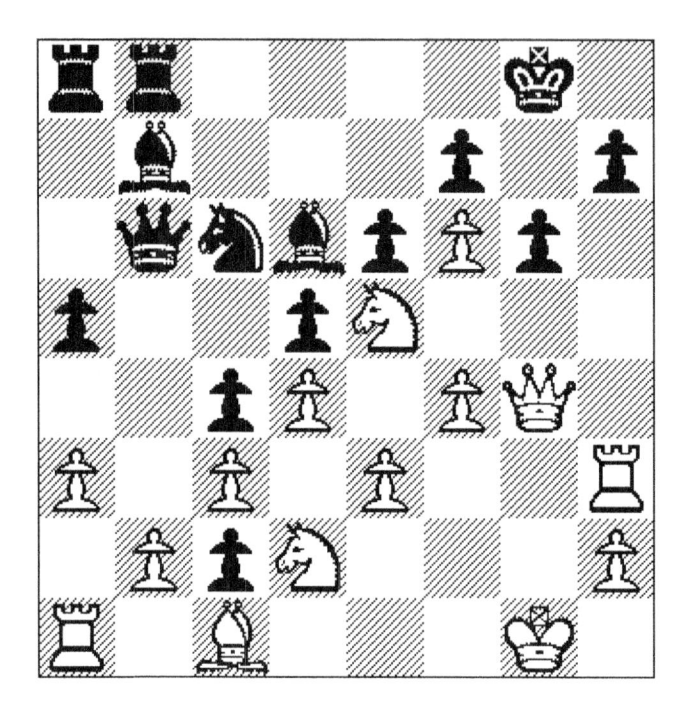

19. Qh4 h5 20. Qg5, followed by Rh5 is imminent.

Ne5

At least getting rid of one attacker.
18...Bf8 19. Nf7!

19. fe5 Bf8 20. Nf3 h6

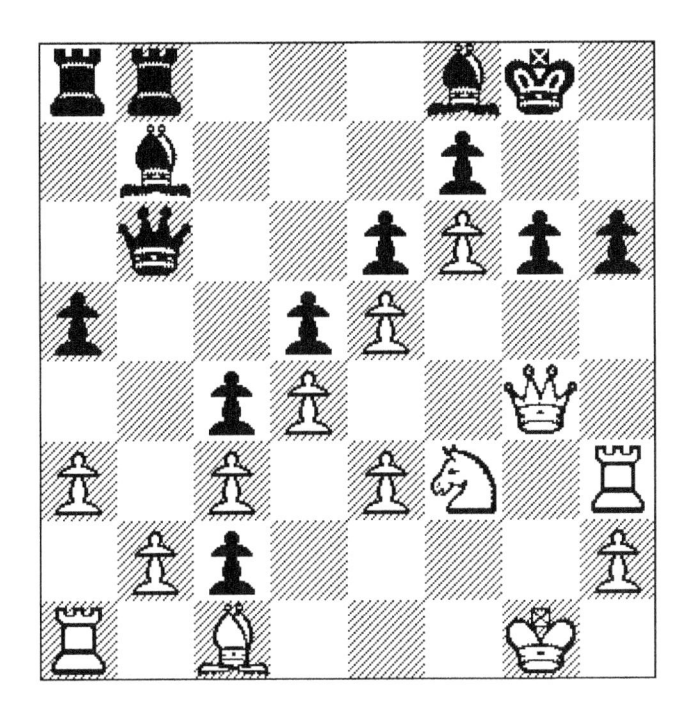

This one is funny.
Stockfish is about to promote, but it gets mated first.

21. Rh4!

White prepares Qh3 and Rh6.
There is no escape.

Bc6 22. Qh3 Qd8

Qb2 Rh6 Bg7 Rh7

23. Ng5

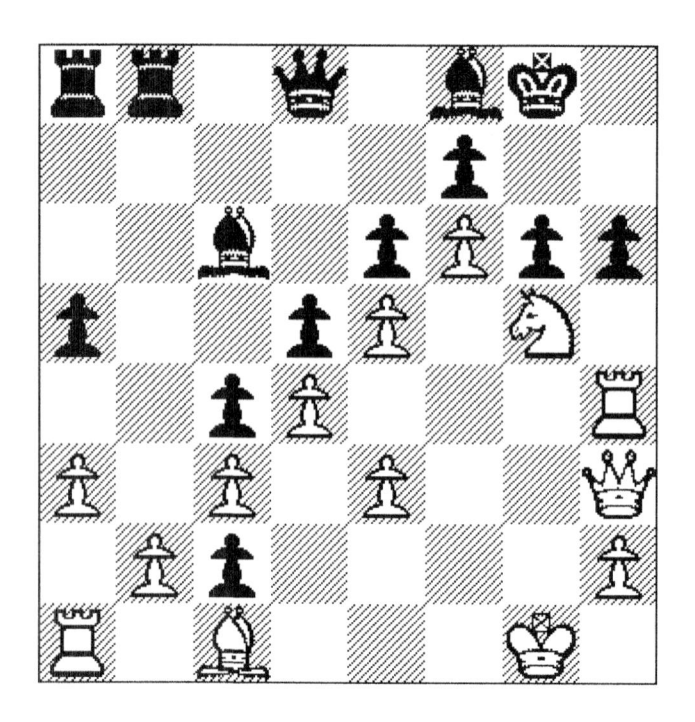

23. Rh6 Bh6 24. Qh6 Qf8 25. Qh4, followed by Ng5, is also possible.

Rb2

An act of desperation. White even does not have to capture the rook.

24. Rh6 Qf6

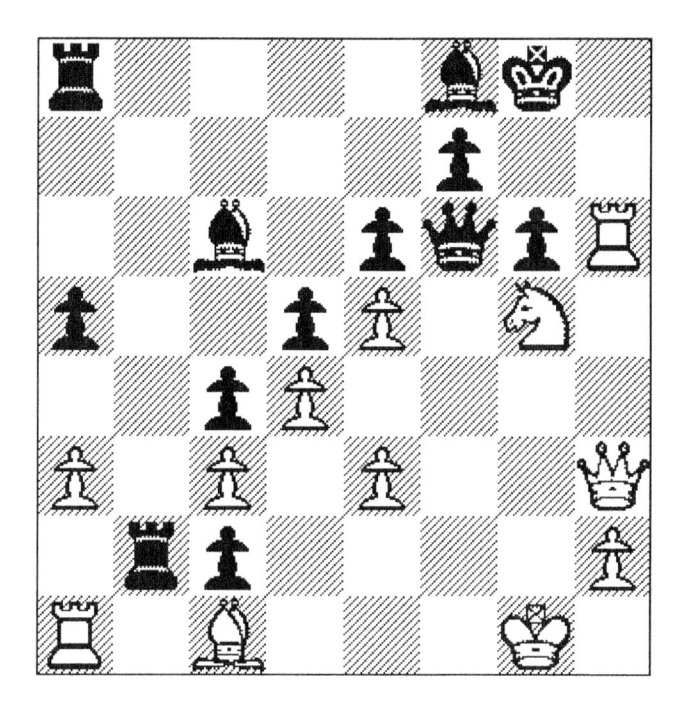

That tells it all.

**25. ef6 Bg7 26. Rh8 Bh8
27. Qh7 Kf8 28. Qf7 mate**

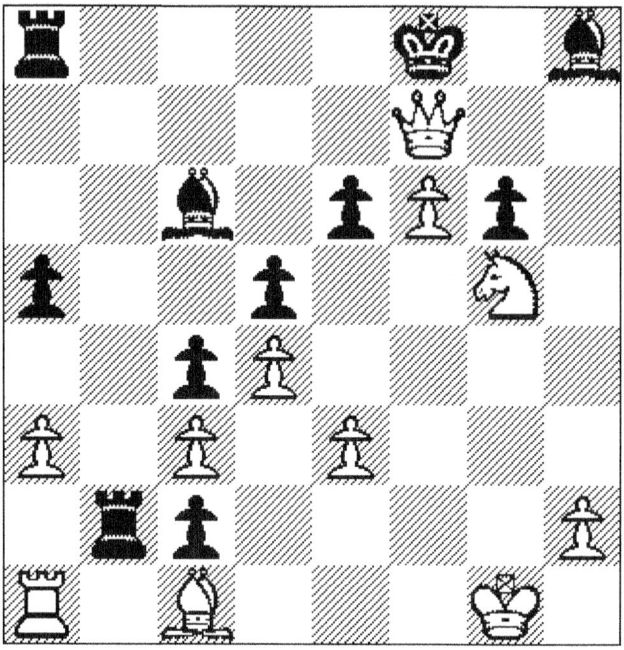

Game 25
Too complicated

June 5th 2014
White: Lyudmil Tsvetkov
Black: Stockfish 5
A07 Reti Opening, King's Indian Attack

**1. d3 d5 2. Nf3 Nf6 3. g3 Nc6
4. Bg2 e5 5. O-O Be7 6. Nc3 d4**

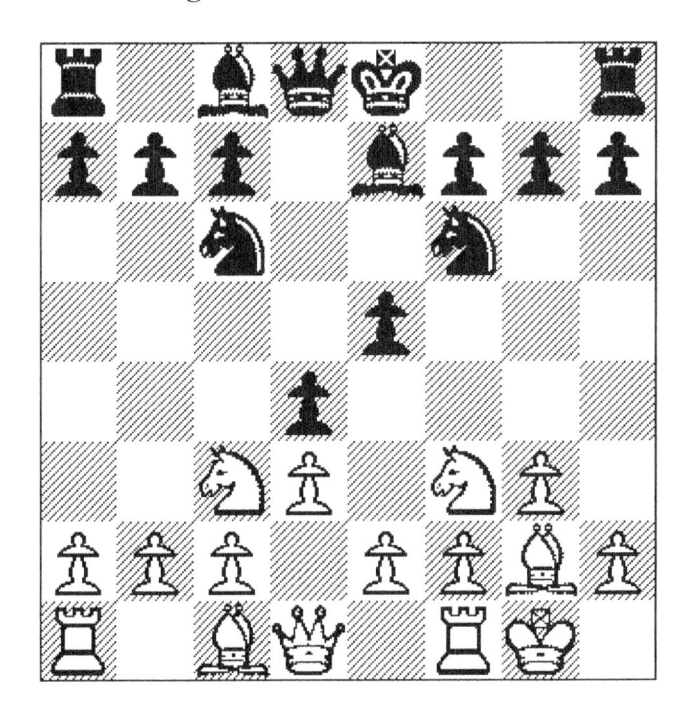

The King's Indian Attack in a slightly revised version.

The knight has to retreat to b1 now, but that is no problem, as e2-e4 will follow soon.

7. Nb1 O-O 8. e4 Be6

de3 Be3 Nd5 might have been preferable, with more or less equal game.

9. Kh1

In order for the knight to go to g1 and push f4.

Nd7 10. Ng1 a5

10...f5 11. ef5 Bf5 12. Nd2 is better for white.

11. f4 f6

If 11...f5 now, white has even 12. ef5 Bf5 13. g4! Be6 14. f5, with quite some edge.
11...ef4 12. gf4 is not an option either.

12. f5 Bf7 13. g4

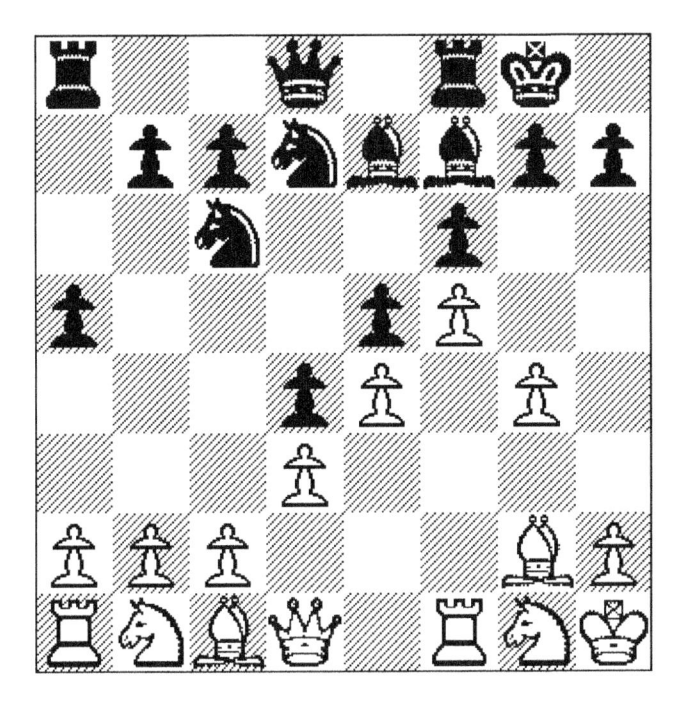

The assault has started. Black has to suffer a lot.

a4 14. h4

a3 was also an option, but this time white is brave and reckless.

b5 15. Nh3 Qe8

So that on g5 black has Bh5.

16. Bf3

Preventing abovementioned possibility.

Kh8 17. g5

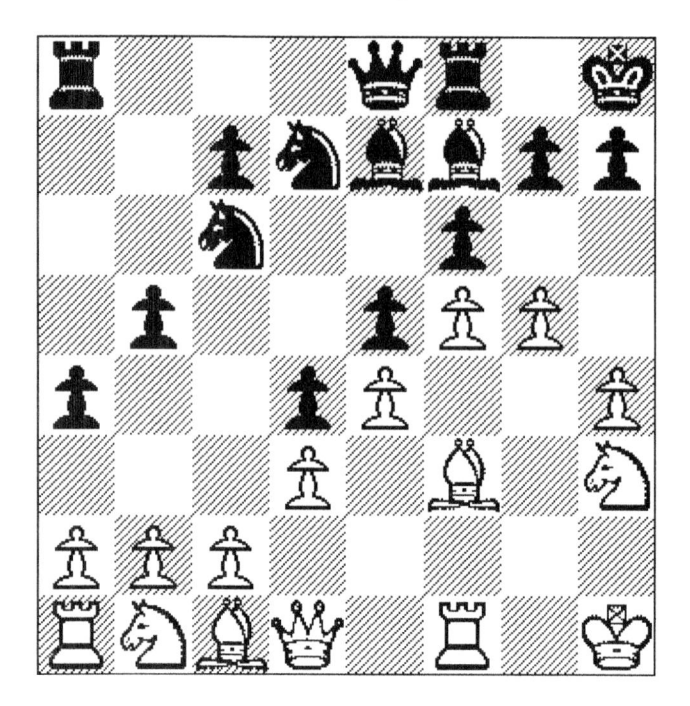

Now, the pawns start rolling.

g6

Both h5 and g6(maybe not now, but after some preparation, Rg1, etc.) are considerable threats, so Stockfish decides to occupy the g6 square.

18. Rg1

The g file is a better location for the rook.

Rg8

Stockfish improves too.

19. Nd2

White should not start a premature attack.

Nc5 20. Nf1 Qd8

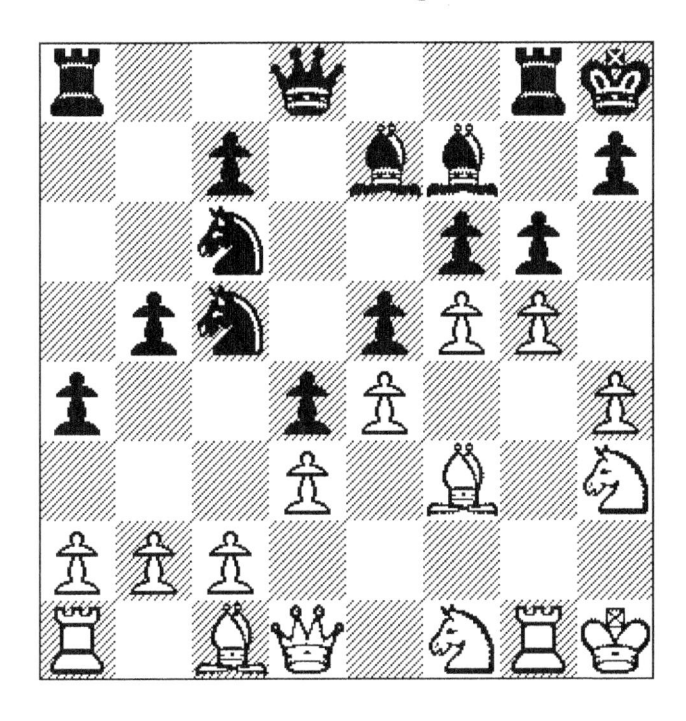

Taking aim at g5 once more, but also defending the f6 square.

The clash of the f5-g6 and g5-f6 pawns fills the air with tension beyond the conceivable.

21. Ng3

Bringing up more reserves.

Be8

Any capture on f5 or g5 will only post there more active white pieces, so Stockfish does not have a plethora of options.

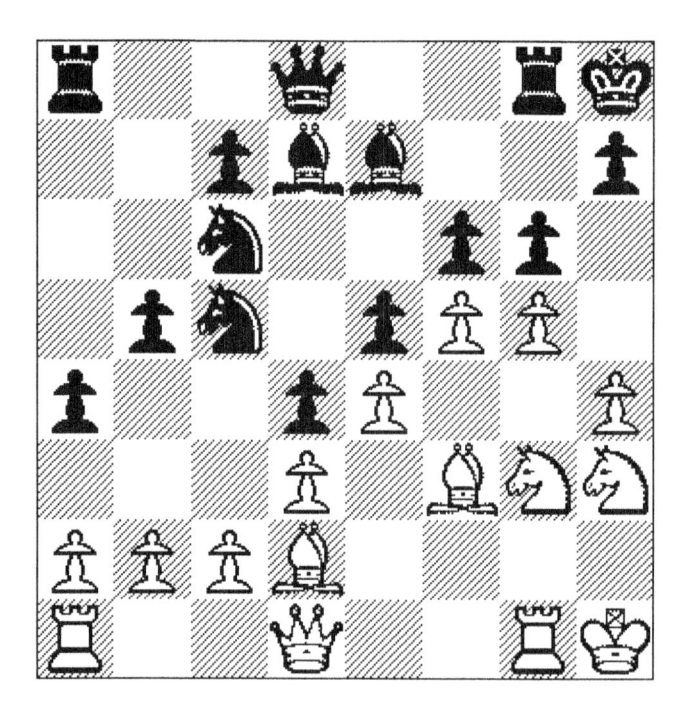

22. Bd2 Bd7

Targeting f5, as well as the knight on h3.

Tactical nuances are always important, no matter the strategic implications.

23. Qe2

Connecting the rooks and developing.

a3

b4, followed by b3, was an alternative, and the position is too complicated to enumerate all variations. White retains a clear edge though.

24. b3

Of course, opening the game should be avoided.

Qf8

The queen comes closer to the king side, where it could be more useful.

25. Raf1

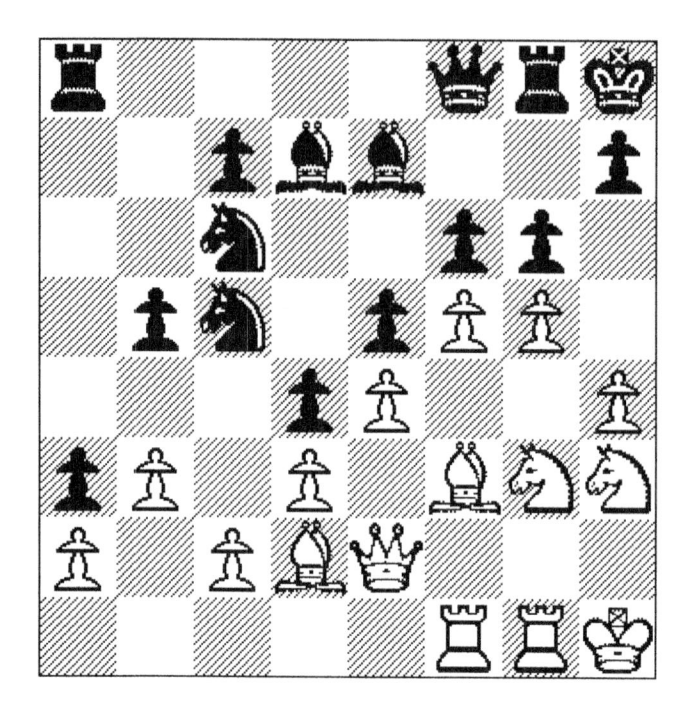

A rook-queen opposition is always a good thing for the rook side.

The position is extremely complicated, both strategically and tactically, I guess everyone will agree.

Bd8

Well, it is difficult to calculate all lines after Qg7 and Raf8.

26. Qh2

The queen switches to the h file and supports the knight on h3.

h5 threatens.

gf5

fg5 hg5(other captures are also possible) is even worse.

27. Nf5

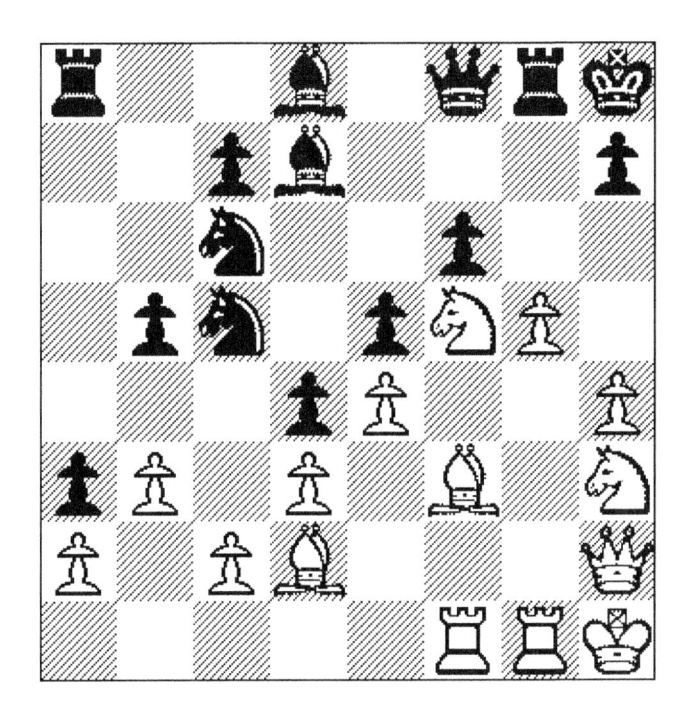

ef5 might have been the better choice.

Too many lines here, so I am unable to explain everything.

People, who wish to do so, might want to check with some top engine.

b4

Ratcheting up space advantage on the queen side.
Good possibilities are not available.
Bf5 ef5 leaves the black knight on c6 en prise.

28. Bh5

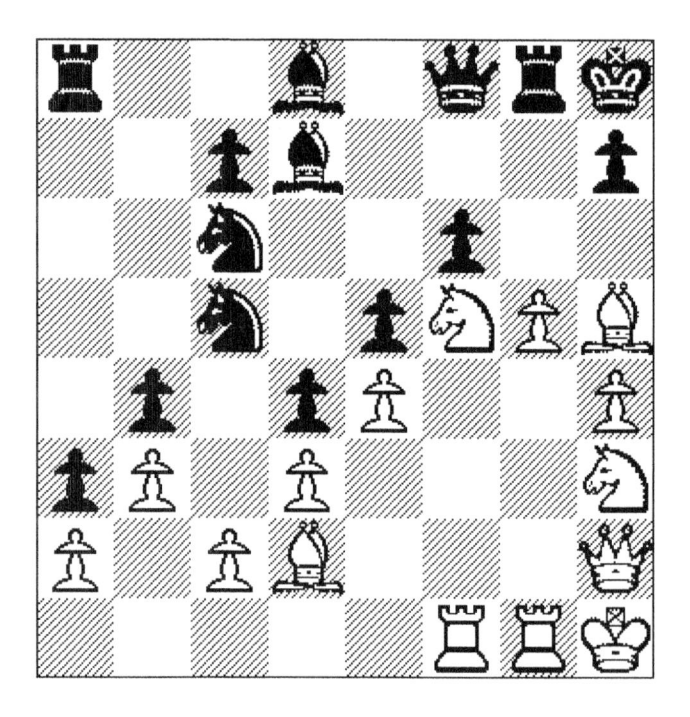

Clearing the f file and envisaging g6.

Bf5

Stockfish does not have much choice.
28...Ne6 29. g6, followed by Bh6
    28...Be8 29. Be8 Qe8 30. gf6 Bf6(Rg1 Rg1 is identical) 31. Rg8 Qg8 32. Rg1 is hopeless too.

29. Rf5

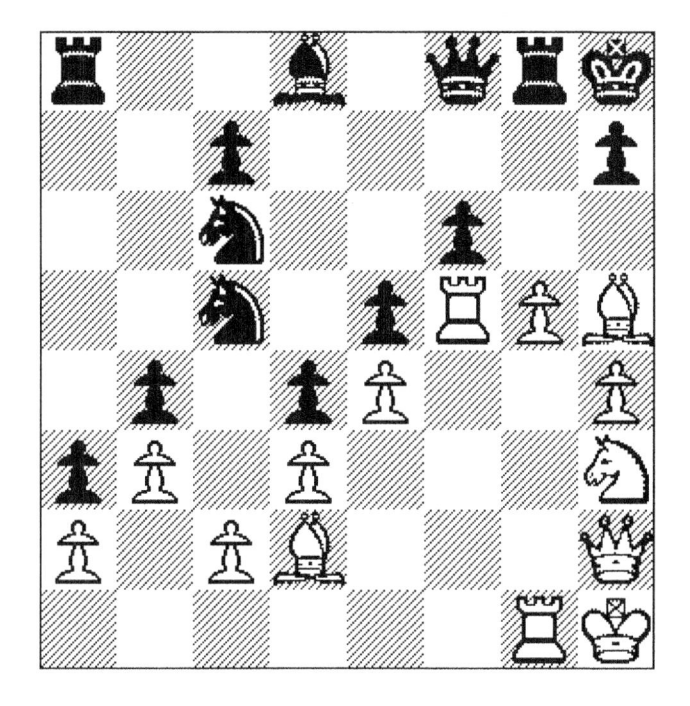

ef5 also wins and might even have been stronger.

Nd7 30. Rff1

Black has been threatening Ne7, attacking the rook, but 30. Rf2(to double rooks on either the f or g file) or 30. gf6 might have been stronger.

Try to play this position against a top engine, to see how easy it is to find the best moves.

Rg7

Well, tactical shuffling.

31. g6

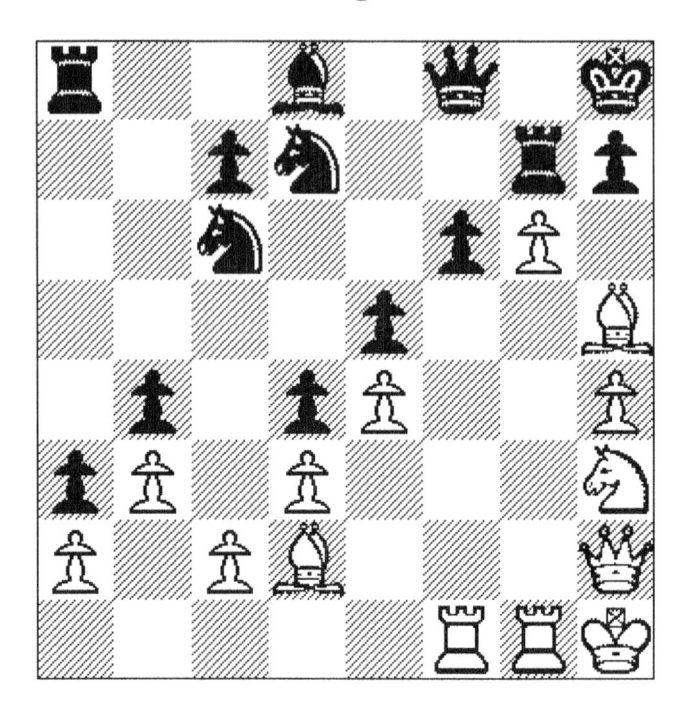

Threatening Bh6.
The rook will fall one way or another.
31...hg6 32. Bg6 Qg8(attacking g6) 33. Qe2 Rg6 34. Qh5

Qe8 32. Bh6?

That dissipates most of white's advantage.
32. Qe2 has been winning much quicker.

Rg6 33. Bg6 hg6

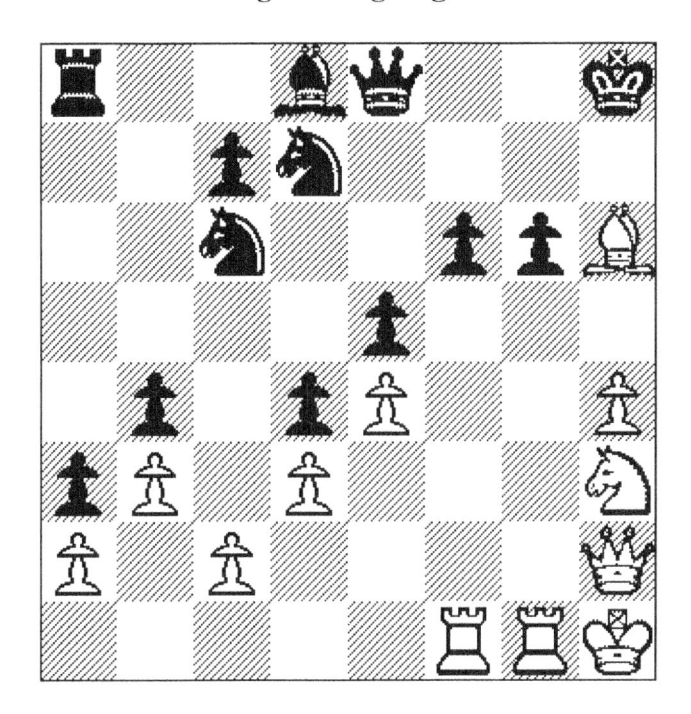

White has an obviously winning position, that is not that easy to win.

With the queen on e2, it could have jumped to g4 straight away.

34. h5

Qe2 was still better.
The queen is too inactive on h2.

g5

Black passes.

Of course, gh5 Bg7 mates quickly.

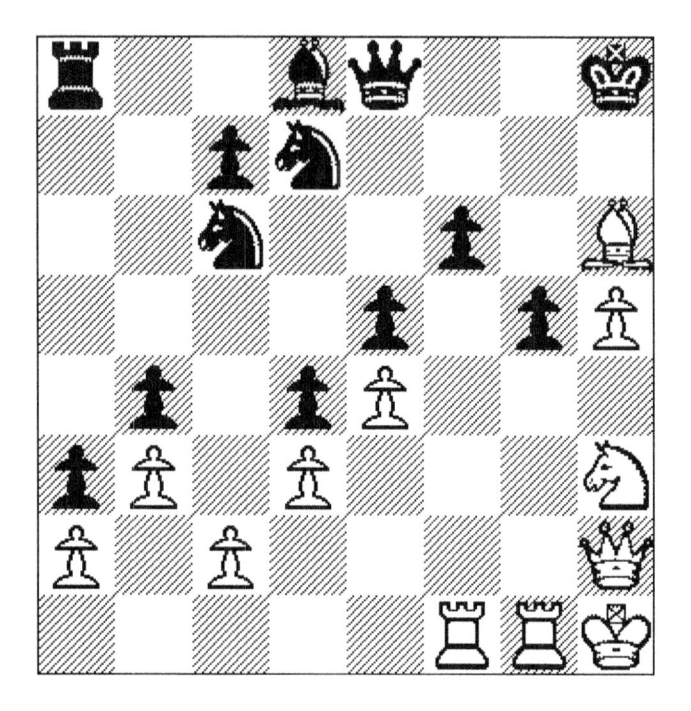

White has to sacrifice something to penetrate.

35. Ng5 fg5 36. Bg5 Bg5 37. Rg5

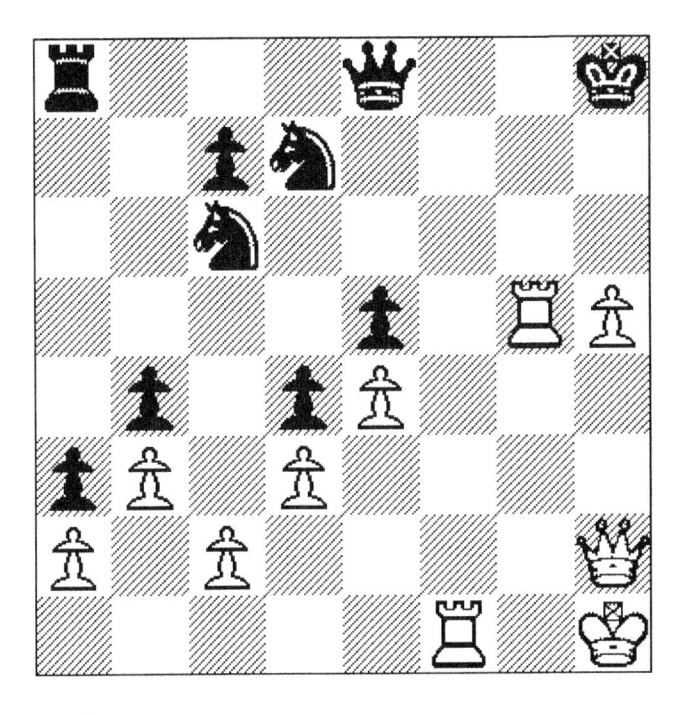

That was more or less forced.
How does now black defend?
Seemingly, impossible.
The black king is too exposed, white has a powerful storming pawn/passer and the black pieces are too uncoordinated.

Ne7

No better alternative.
37...Nf8 38. Rg6! should be even weaker.

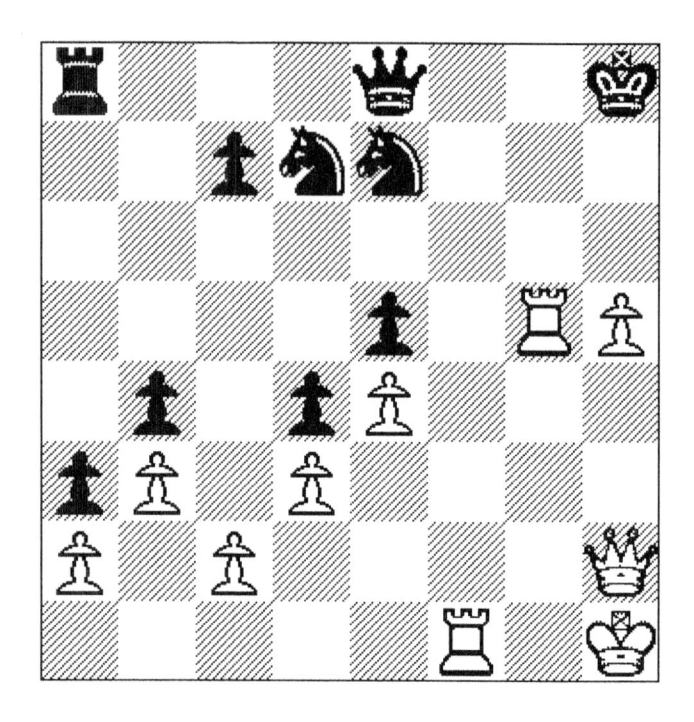

38. Rg6?

Unnecessarily complicates things.

38. Re5! was winning on the spot, for example 33...Ne5 34. Qe5 check Kh7(Kg8 Rg1) 35. Rf6(threatening Re6) Ng8(Qd8 Rf7) 36. Qf5 check Kh8(Kg7 h6) 37. Rf7

Ng8 39. Rfg1 Qf7

If Ndf6, then Qg3-g5.

40. Qh3

To prevent the check on h3.

Ngf6 41. Qf5

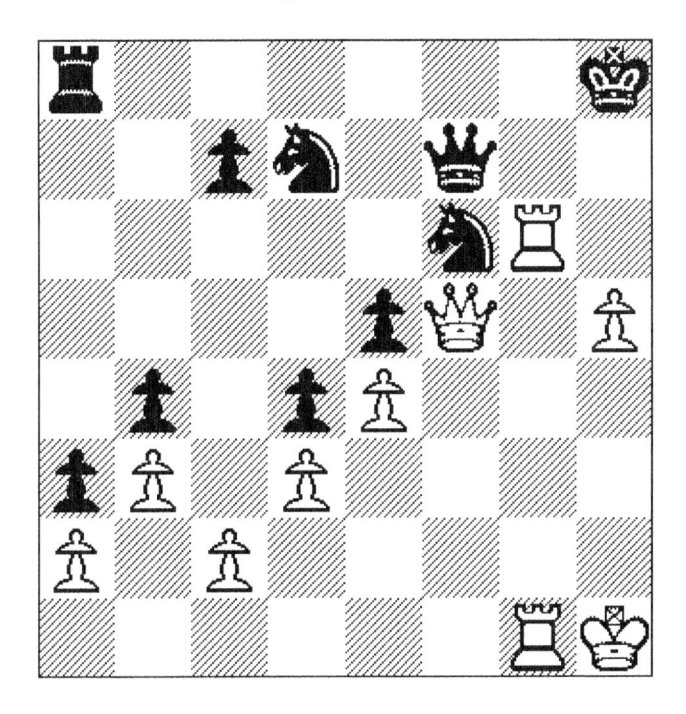

The black pieces are completely tied and awfully passive.

Rh6 threatens.

Winning is just a matter of time.

Qf8

Or 41...Rf8 42. h6(other continuations are also possible), followed by Rg7, and black is in zugzwang.

The knight on f6 can not retreat, as otherwise it is lost after Qf7 Rf7 and a check on g8.

Even if miraculously black succeeds in changing queens and a pair of rooks, the ensuing endgame is easily won for the rook side against the knight pair, as the knights are too slow in the endgame and the rook will pick up most of the black pawns on the queen side.

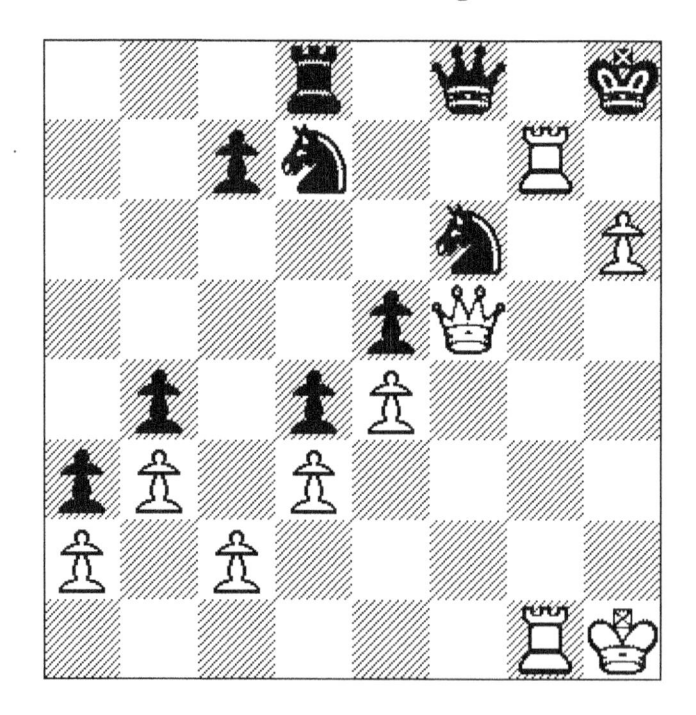

42. h6 Rd8 43. Rg7

Black is completely helpless.

The knight on f6 can not budge because of mate on h7, and white threatens Qg6 and Rf7.

Re8 44. Qg6 Re7 45. Re7

1-0

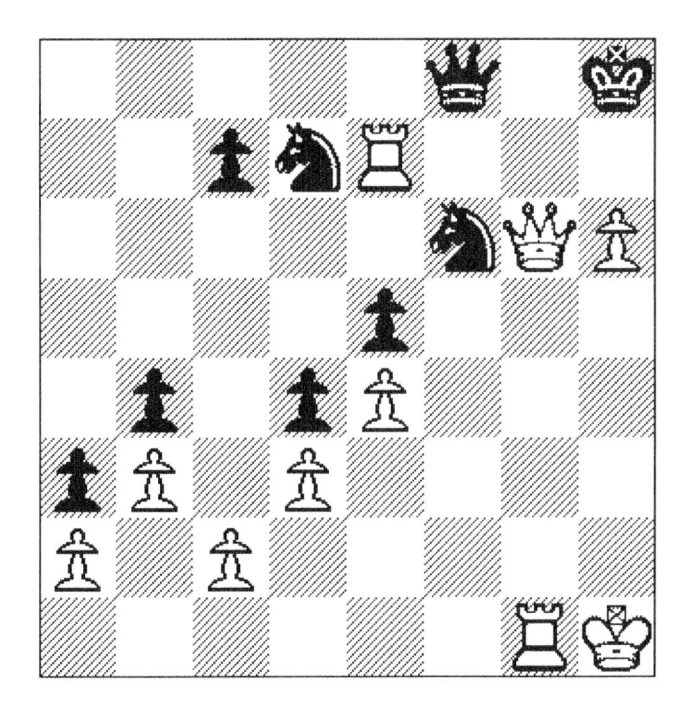

After 45...Qe7 46. Qg7 Qg7 47. Rg7, black is in zugzwang and the white king slowly penetrates to f5.

161

Game 26
Blunder Stockfish

June 7th 2014
White: Lyudmil Tsvetkov
Black: Stockfish 5
D05 Queen's Pawn Game, Colle System

1. e3

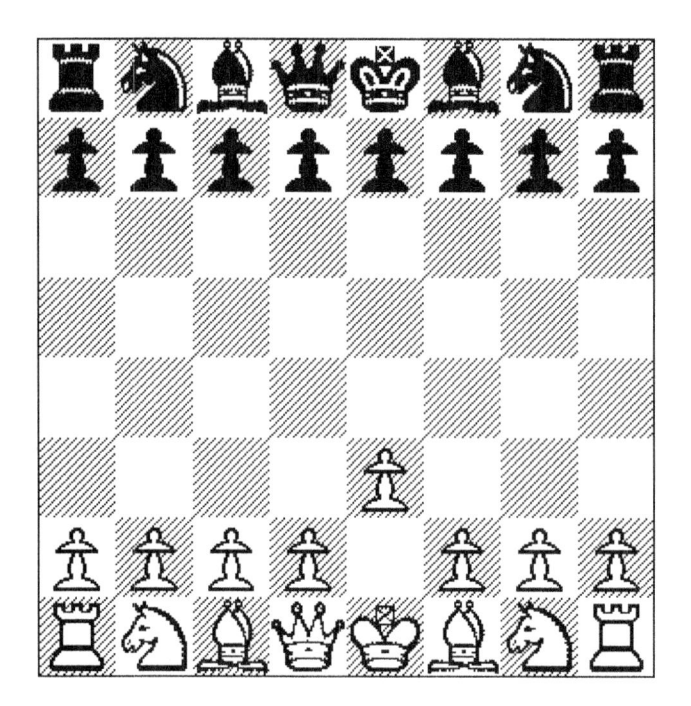

Not that bad, is it?
At least, does not lose.

Nf6

Interesting, that Stockfish does not find the best move, 1...e5 2. d4 ed4(e4 d5) 3. ed4 d5, with complete equality.

Obviously, top engines still have too much to learn in the opening.

2. d4 e6 3. Nf3 Be7

Stockfish continues with dubious moves in unchartered waters.

3...d5 straight might have been a bit better.

4. Bd3 d5 5. O-O O-O 6. Ne5

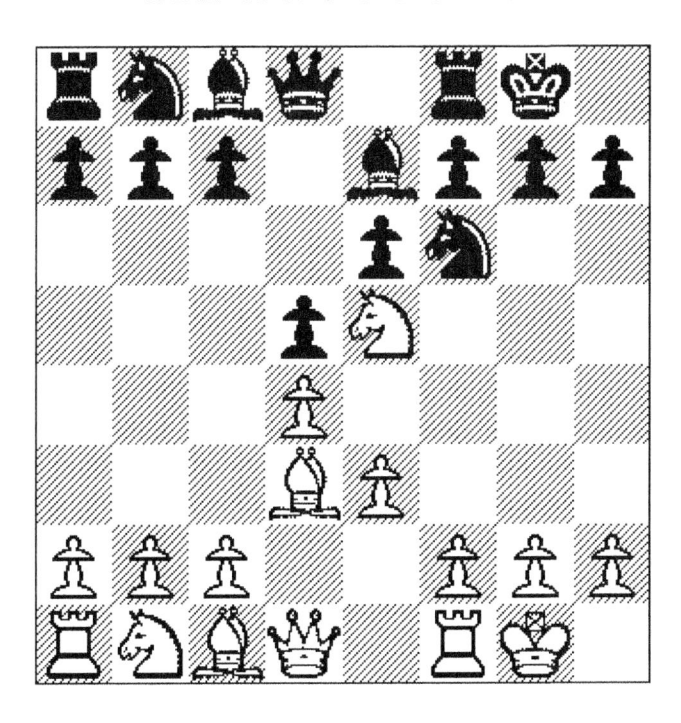

White already has gained some space.

Passive, as it might seem, this system has its venom.

c5 7. c3

Defending d4 a second time. You never know with what pawn it will be indicated to capture there.

Nbd7

Nc6 still seems better.

8. Nd2

Protecting the e4 square once more, so the black knight can not jump there.

Qc7

Another inaccuracy.

Black should have captured on e5, 8...Ne5, and after 9. de5 Nd7 10. f4(Qh5 g6 and Ne5) f5, black should hold that.

After white plays f2-f4, taking on e5 already becomes quite a problem, as white is sufficiently developed.

9. f4 b6 10. g4

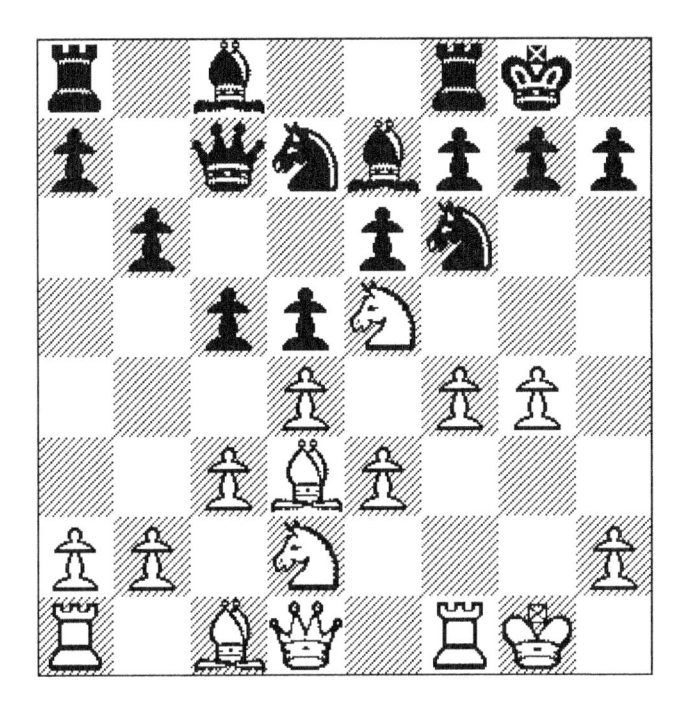

Indeed, white has even the time to flank-storm!

The advantage of that side, even a bigger one, is undisputable.

Bb7

Stockfish threatens with Ne4.

11. Qf3

Preventing that.

g6 12. g5 Ne5

Deciding to capture early on e5. 12...Nh5, as played in similar setups, might have been better.

13. fe5

de5 d4! is a major mistake, of course.

Nh5 14. Qg4

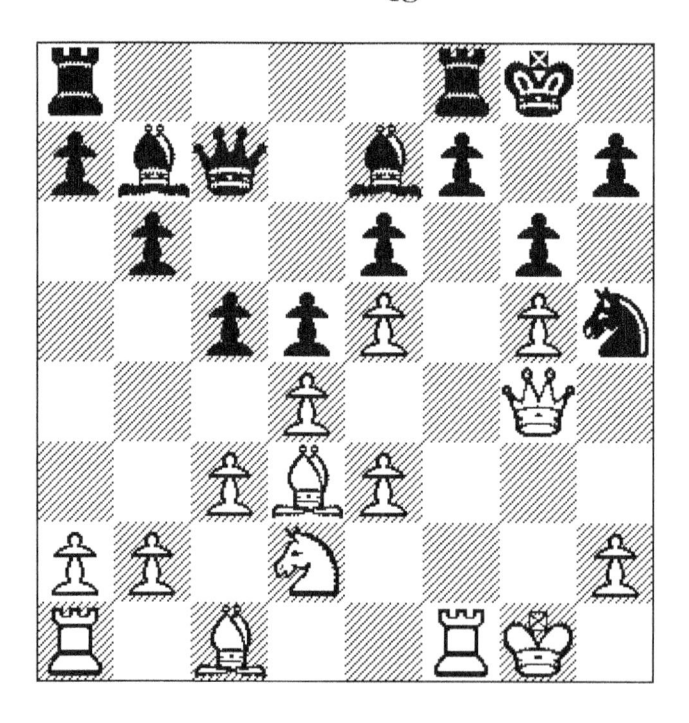

Indeed, the early bind on f7 is intolerable.

Ng7

Stockfish heads to f5.

15. Nf3 Nf5 16. h4

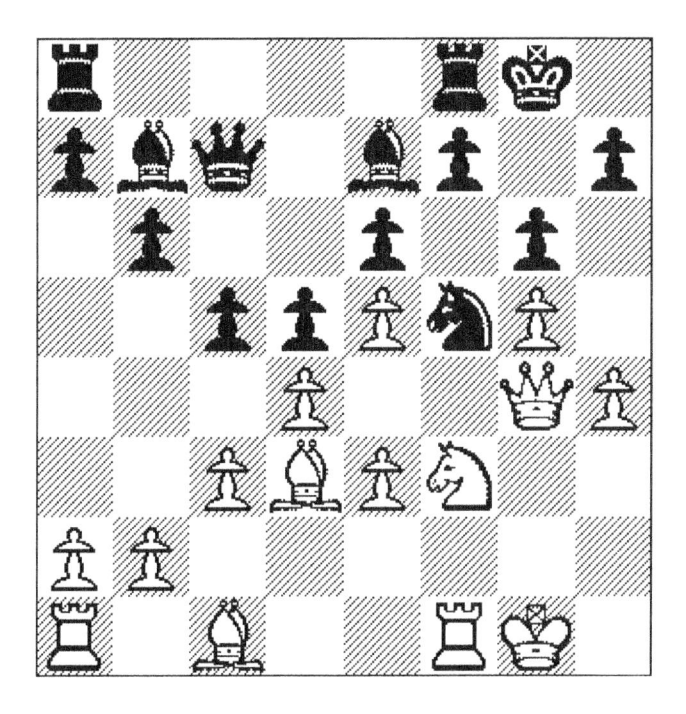

This time, an early h4 is played.
White will try to open the h file as soon as possible.

Qc8 17. Rf2

Stockfish has been threatening Ba6, with exchange of light-square bishops, and the rook leaves the f1 square, so the d3 bishop can retreat to c2, after Ba6 is played(otherwise, black will take on f1).

Ng7?

To f5 or h5?

Stockfish is unrecognisable in this game.

Such an inconsequential approach can hardly bear good fruit.

Even 17...Kg7 18. h5 Rh8 has been preferable.

18. h5!

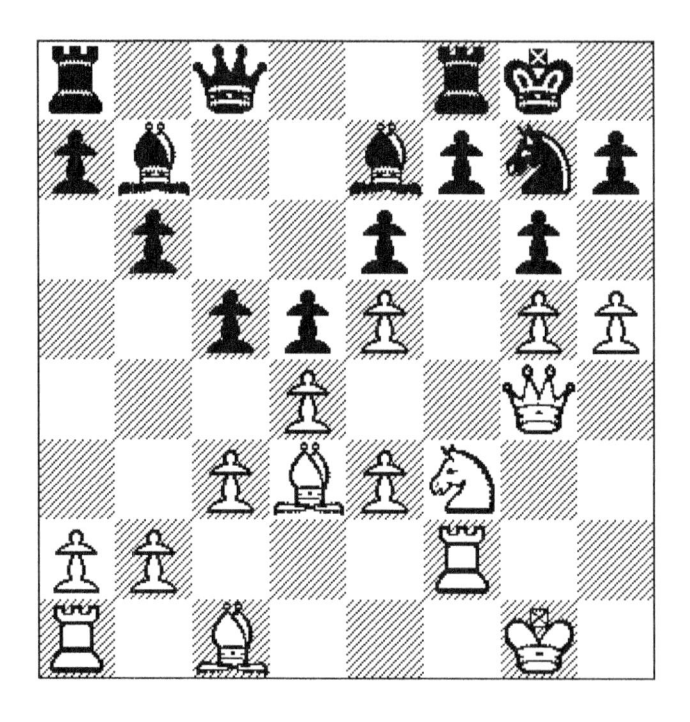

Rh2 Nh5, and the long-winding winning strategy begins again.

Now, white should be able to break through much quicker.

Nh5

gh5 is even worse.

19. Rh2

Rh5 already threatens.

Qe8

To meet Rh5 gh5 Qh5 with f5.

20. Bd2

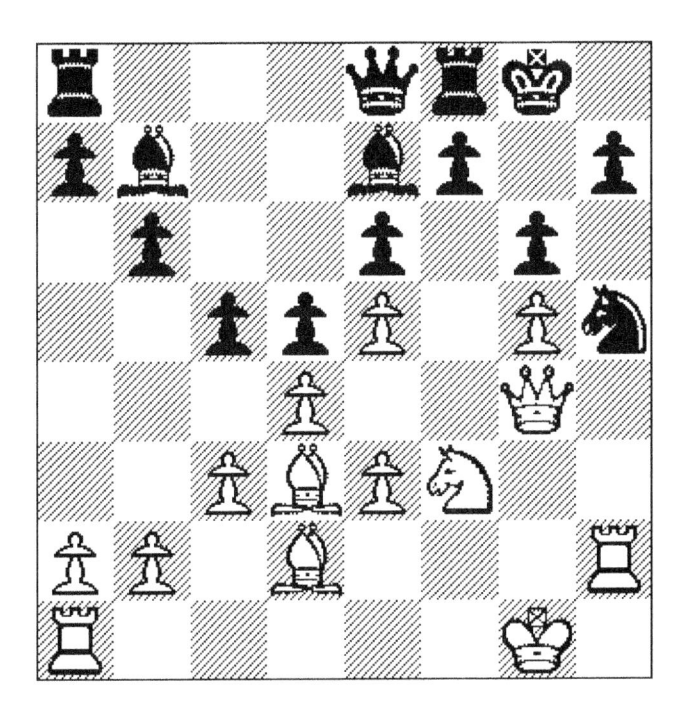

White does not fall for the trick and simply develops.

After the second rook comes to the h file, the game is over.

a5

Ba6 is still a hope.

21. Kg2

Clearing the first rank.

Ng7

21...Kg7 does not help, as after 22. Rh5 gh5 23. Qh5 f5(Rh8 Qh6 check, followed by Rh1) 24. gf6, the pawn takes on f6 with check.

22. Rh6!

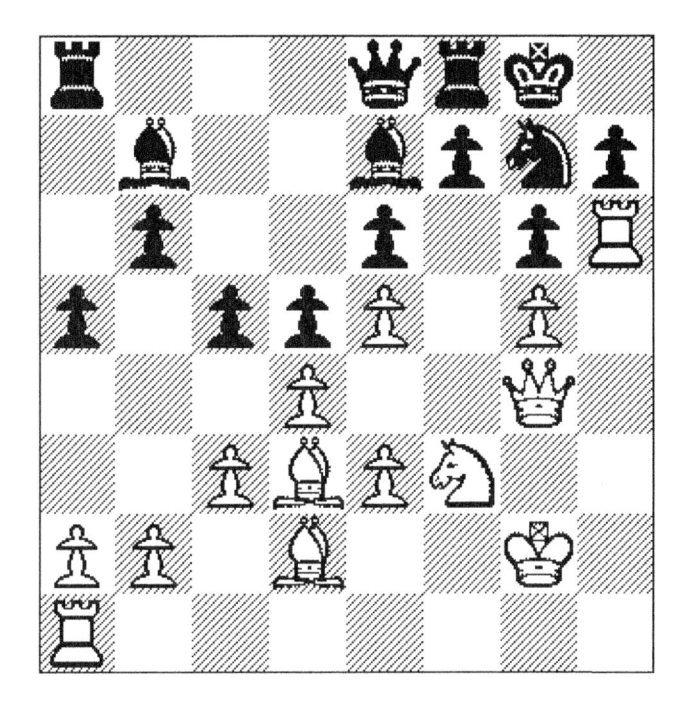

It is not necessary to significantly complicate things after 22. Rah1 h5! 23. gh6 Nf5.

The rook has blocked the h pawn, making the h5 thrust impossible.

Nf5

Simply no other moves.

23. Bf5 Qb5

ef5 Qh4, with mate in a couple of moves.
Now, Qe2 check threatens.

24. Kf2

It's difficult to find a non-winning move.

cd4 25. ed4 Bc6 26. Qh4

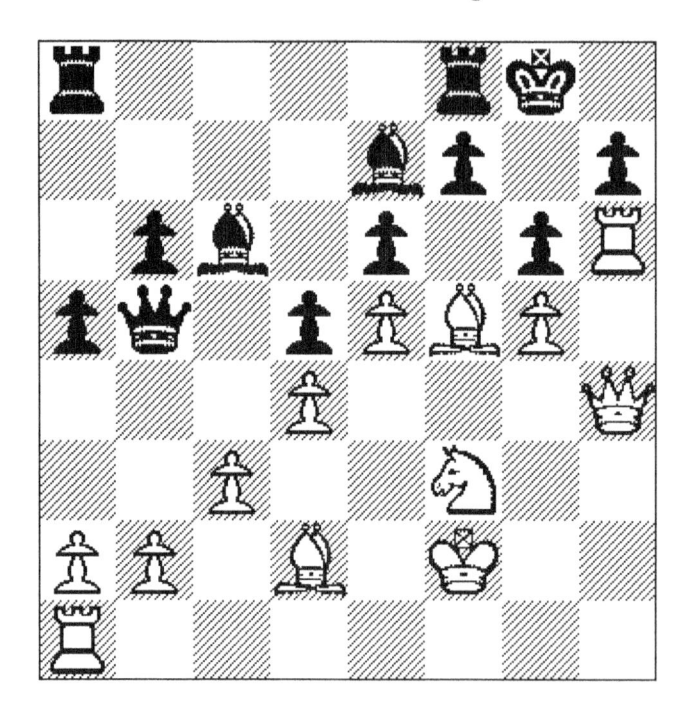

Stockfish resigned.

It is difficult to imagine a more convincing win on the part of the human and a weaker play on the part of the engine.

At some point, I wanted to check if this game has indeed been played by Stockfish, but my database says so.

Seemingly, top engines only regress with newer editions.

Game 27
Fully blocked

February 6th 2015
White: Lyudmil Tsvetkov
Black: Stockfish 6
D00 Queen's Pawn Game

**1. f4 Nf6 2. Nf3 e6 3. d4 d5
4. e3 c5 5. c3 Be7 6. Bd3 O-O
7. O-O**

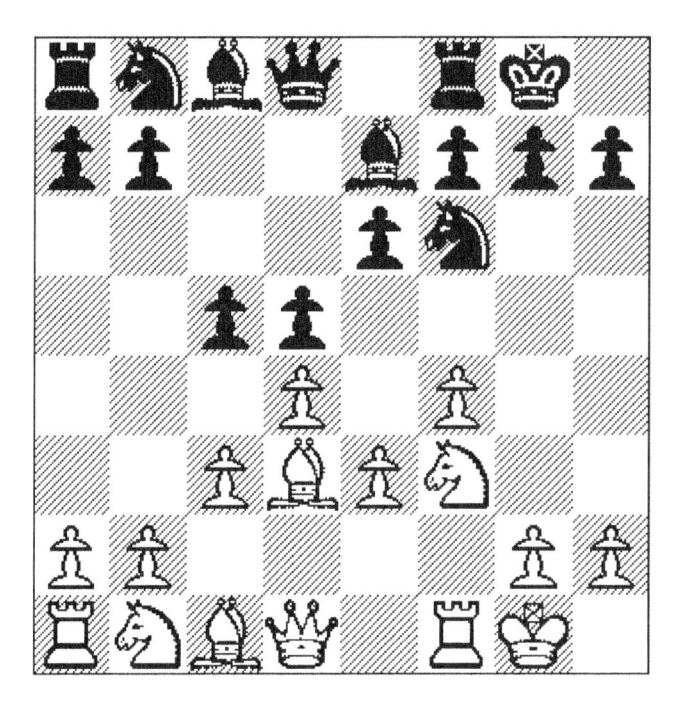

Another Bird-Queen's Pawn Game-Stonewall Attack.

c4

Stockfish opts for an early closure.

**8. Bc2 b5 9. a3 Bb7
10. Ne5 a5**

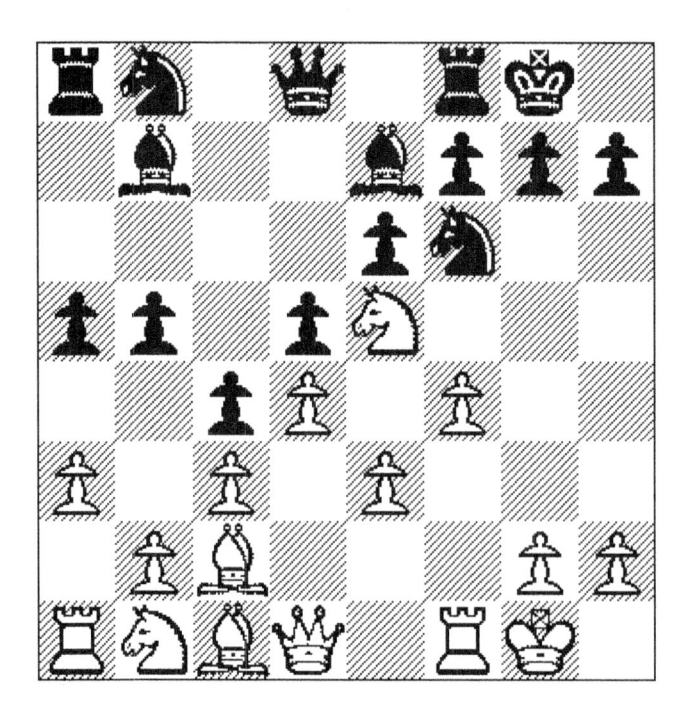

10...Ne4 has been the much better move again.

11. Nd2 a4

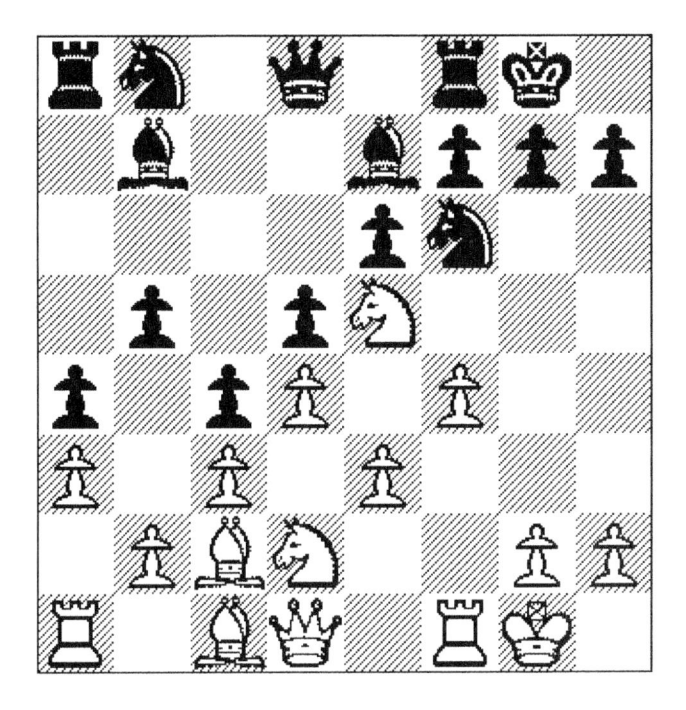

Now, this is a surprise.

Stockfish closes completely the game on the queen side.

While it is difficult to call this a straightforward mistake(black can bring a mighty attacking knight to the 6th rank after Nc6-a5-b3), the complete lack of counterplay is certainly not a good choice.

Obviously, the engine's space advantage parameters are not well-tuned for this particular type of position.

12. Qf3 Nc6 13. g4

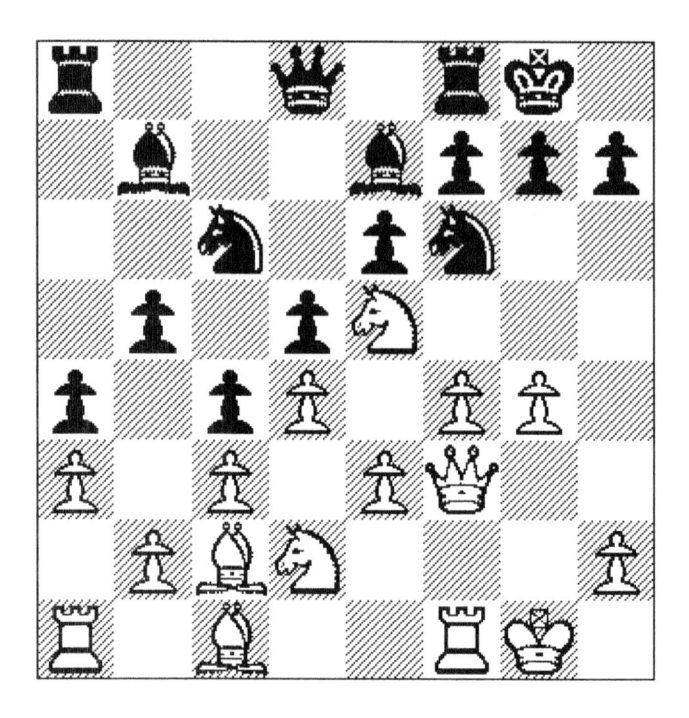

The assault has started.

g6 14. g5 Ne5

Preferring an early capture on e5, making use of the fact, that taking with the f pawn very much suits black after 15. fe5 Ne4!(the g5 pawn is weak) 16. Ne4 de4 17. Be4 Be4 18. Qe4 Bg5.

15. de5 Nd7

Nh5 might have been a bit preferable, but Stockfish has Nc5-d3/e4/b3 in mind.

Opening the game with d4 is impossible, as the bishop on b7 is unprotected.

16. Qg4 Nc5 17. Nf3

Heading to d4 to completely close the game and deprive black of any tactical counterplay based on d5-d4.

Look how one can close a position not only by blocking enemy pawns, but also by attacking twice the square in front of them(as the b5 pawn is), or by blocking them with pieces(as the d4 knight will soon block the d5 pawn).

Qb6 18. Nd4

Mission completed.
An interesting position, is not it?

Ne4 19. Rf3

Rook lift can hardly be a bad move.

Bc6 20. Rh3

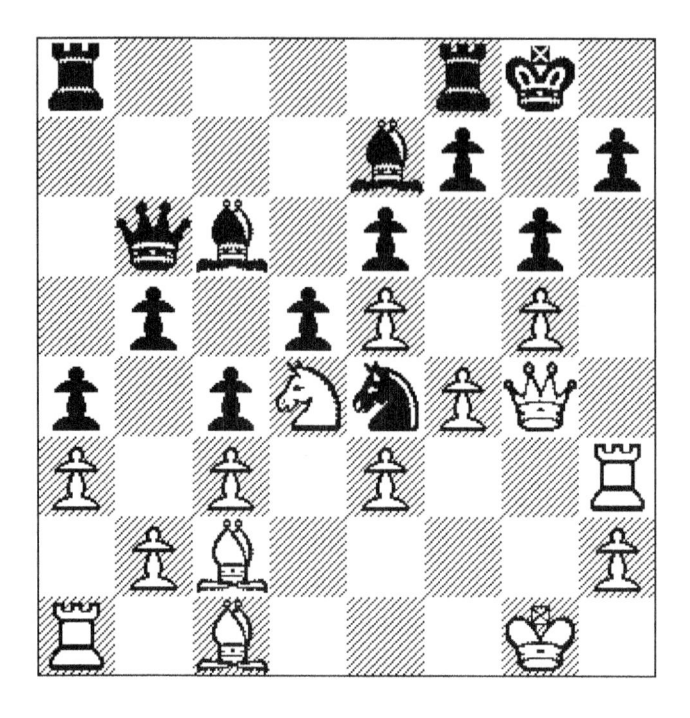

Of course, white is not tempted to capture on c6.
The centrally posted knight is much more valuable than the self-blocked bishop.

Rfc8 21. Qe2

A strong retreat. The queen will support the dark-square bishop to develop to d2.
21. Qh4 h5
21. Rh6 Bf8 and the rook must go back.

Qd8 22. Bd2 Qf8

The queen will try to defend the h7 square.

23. Kh1

Evacuating the g1 square for the queenside rook.

Nc5

Nd2 Qd2 is no option.

Black lacks any realistic plan, while white's plan is clear, to bring more forces to the king side and attack the h7 square.

24. Rg1 Ne4

Indeed, Stockfish has started shuffling.

25. Rg4

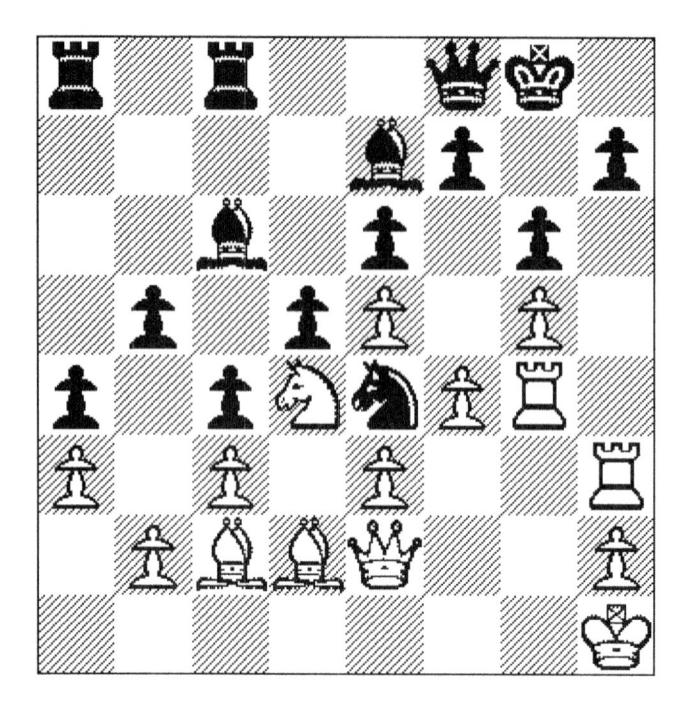

The rook heads to h4.

Qg7

Prophylactically defending h7.
The assault will come one way or another.

26. Be1

To free the queen from the uncharacteristic duty of protecting the bishop. It will soon be needed elsewhere.

Qh8

A mysterious move, whose purpose is to clear the f8-h6 diagonal, so that Rh6 is met by Bf8.

27. Rgh4

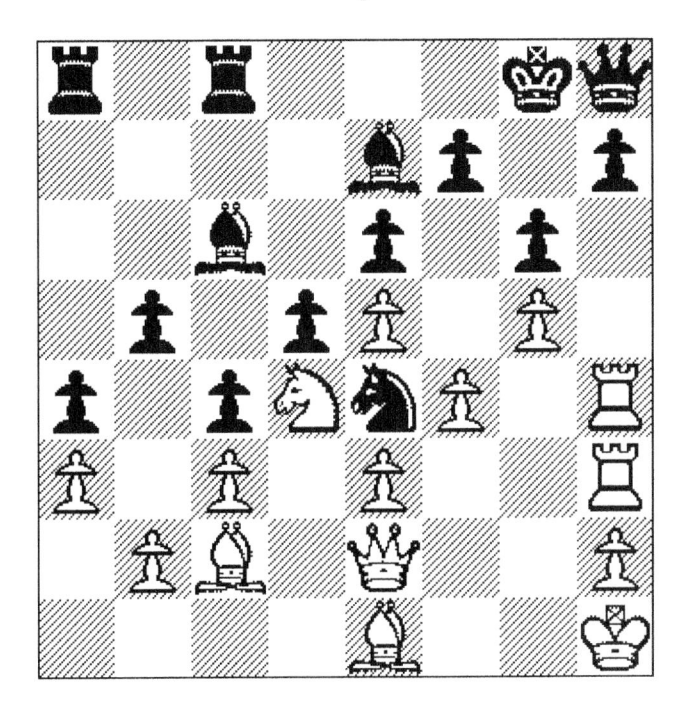

It is difficult to imagine how one side might be more passive than what black is.

Still, nothing concrete is seen.

Bd7

Getting away from the knight attack.

27...h5 is a mistake, as after 28. Bd1!(targeting h5), followed by Qg2 and Bh5, white crashes in.

28. Bd1

The bishop will never capture on e4, so it changes trajectory.

28. Rh7 Qh7 29. Rh7 Kh7 is weak, as white has draw at most, if it manages to close the position.

Rd8 29. Qg2 Rac8

As noted, h5 is met by Bh5.

30. Rh6

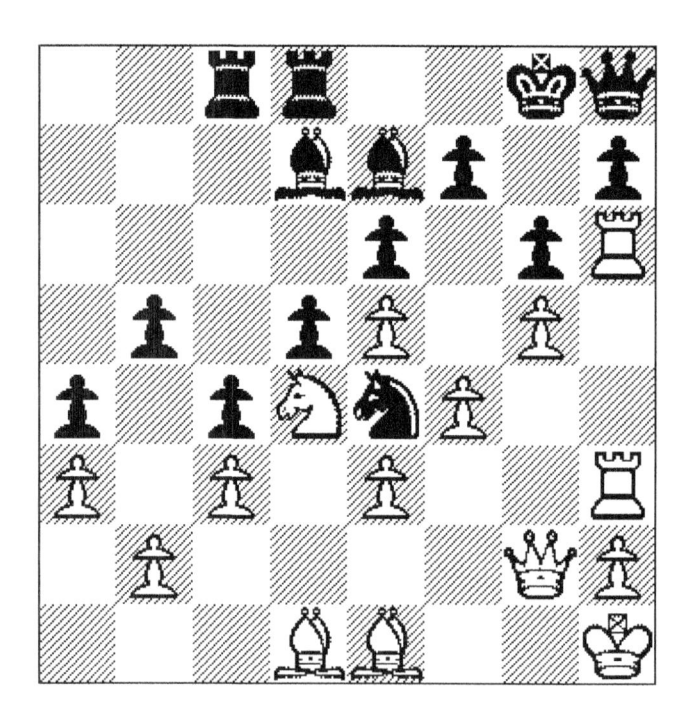

Winning a little time.
Let's see, if Stockfish will drive away the rook.

Qg4-h4 threatens.

Bf8

The engine is obstinate.

31. R6h4 Be7

Expecting a three-fold.

32. Kg1

Not this time.
Under time pressure, I myself am expecting Stockfish to blunder.

Nc5

The knight on d3 will be even more active.

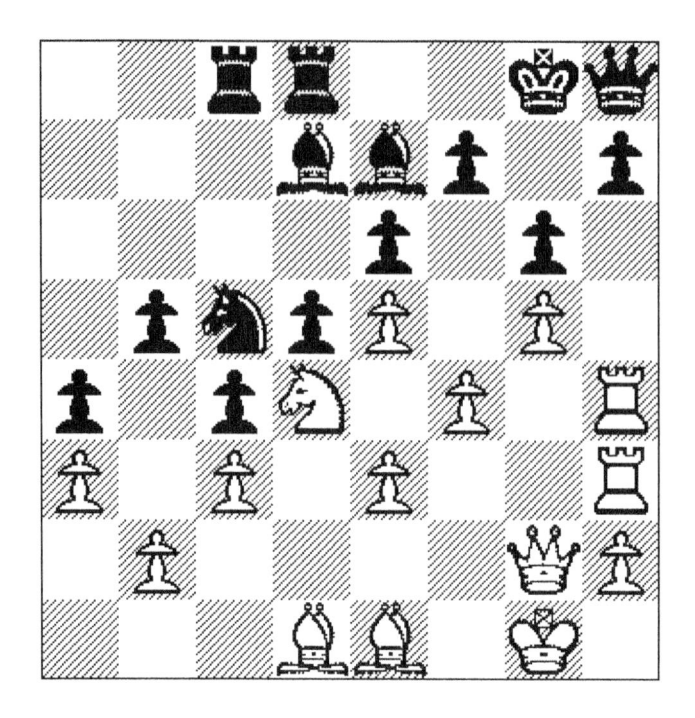

With the present configuration, because of lack of sufficient space on the king side to conduct activities, white seemingly can not win.

The win is there, of course. White should have continued 33. Rg4! Nd3 34. Kf1(protecting the bishop on e1), followed by Rf3, h4, h5, and only then Rg4-h4, Rf3-h3, with a bust.

I, however, does not see that.

Luckily, Stockfish blunders soon.

Under time pressure and in difficult positions, top engines blunder tactically too.

33. Bc2? Rb8 34. Bd2 h5??

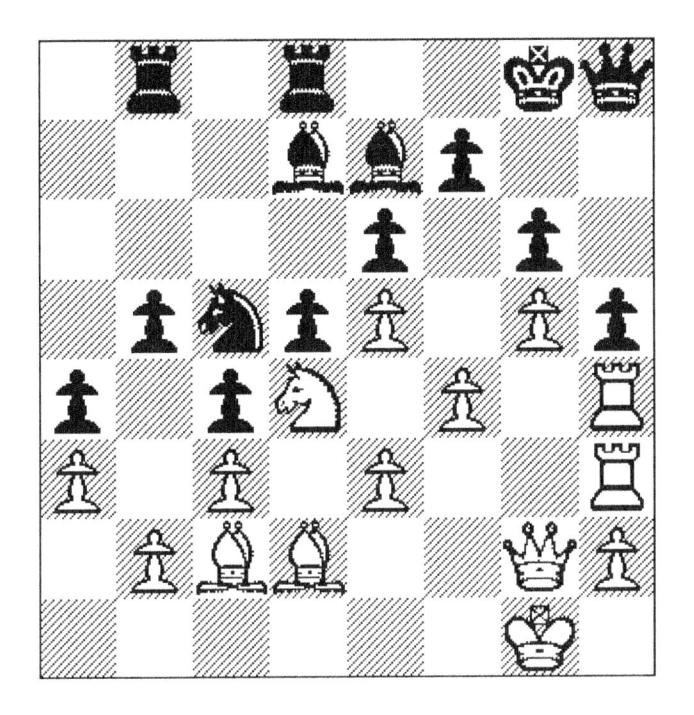

34...Nd3 35. Bd3 cd3 was the much preferable choice.

Now, 35. gh6 Bh4 is impossible, but white has much better.

35. Bd1!

Attacking h5.

Qg7

Nothing better.

36. Bh5 b4

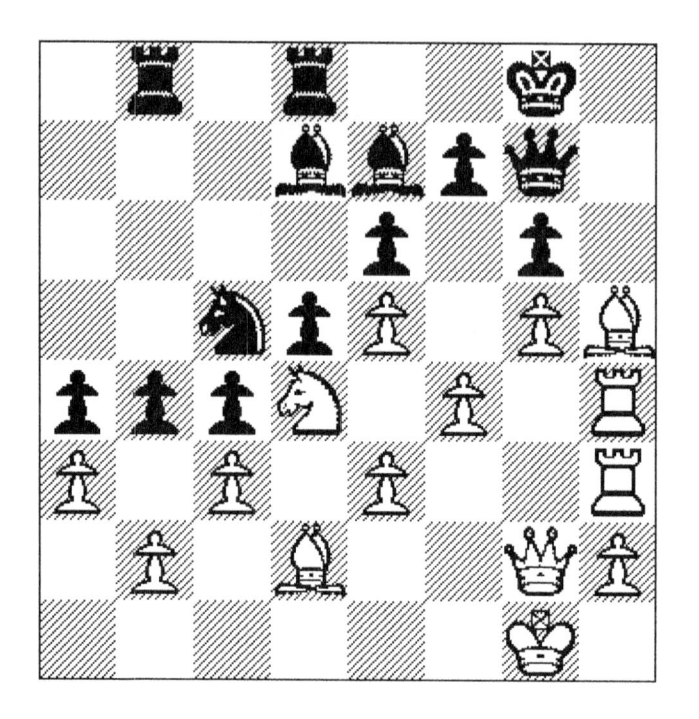

Stockfish clearly understands its position is hopeless and goes on a sacrificial run.

36...gh5 37. Rh5 Qg6(otherwise white plays Qg4-h4) 38. f5 gf5 39. Rh6 Qg7(Qg5 Rg3) 40. g6, with a rout.

37. ab4 Nd3 38. Be2 a3

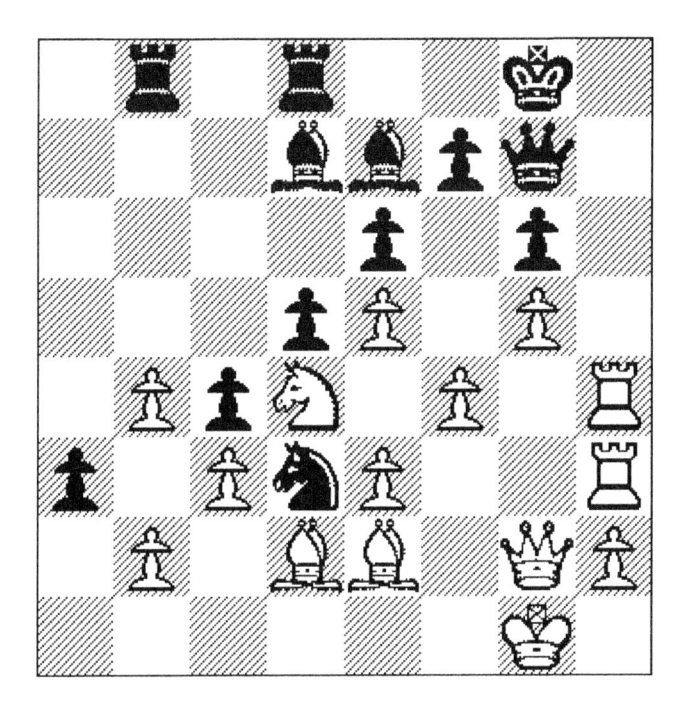

Stockfish prepares to promote.

39. ba3 Bc5

That is already too much.
The engine can not prevent Rh6, Qg4-h4.

40. Rh6

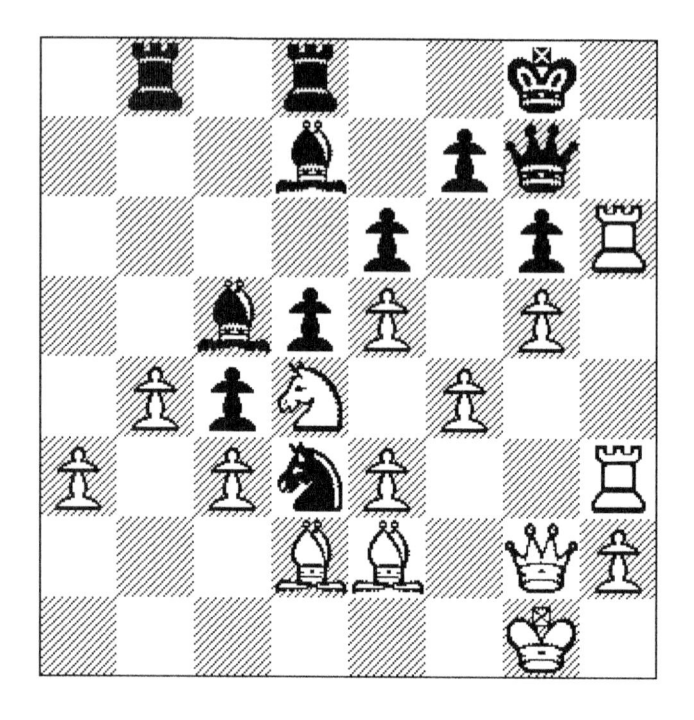

After 40. bc5? Rb1 41. Bf1 Rdb8, black gets too active.

Bd4 41. ed4 Ra8 42. Qg4

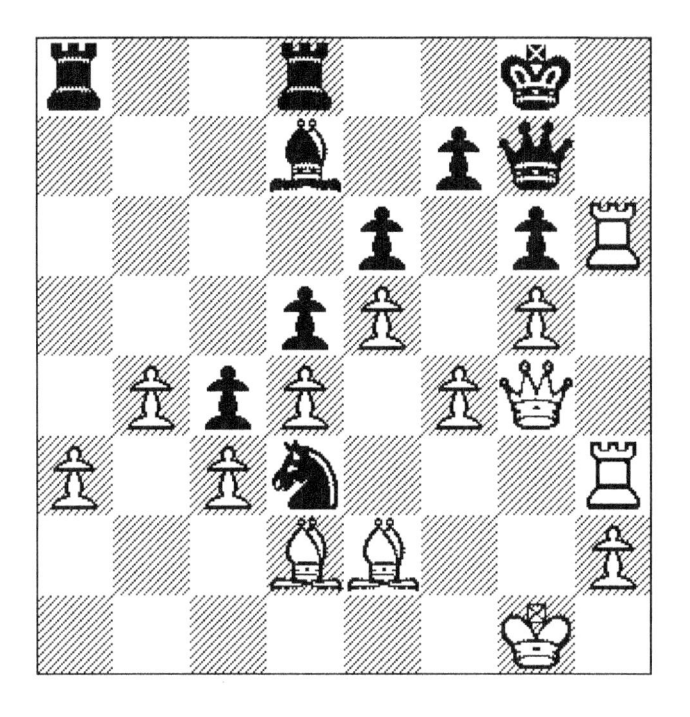

Qh4 mates, at least the black queen.

**Ra3 43. Qh4 Kf8
44. Rh7 Qg8 45. Rh8**

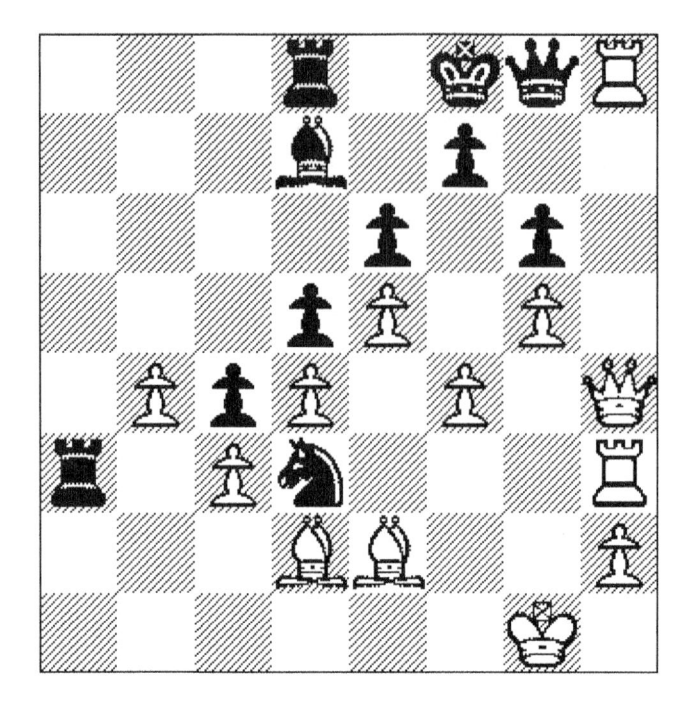

Its royalty is harshly mistreated.

Ke7 46. Rg8 Rg8 47. Qh7

Attacking the rook.

Rf8 48. Bd3

1-0

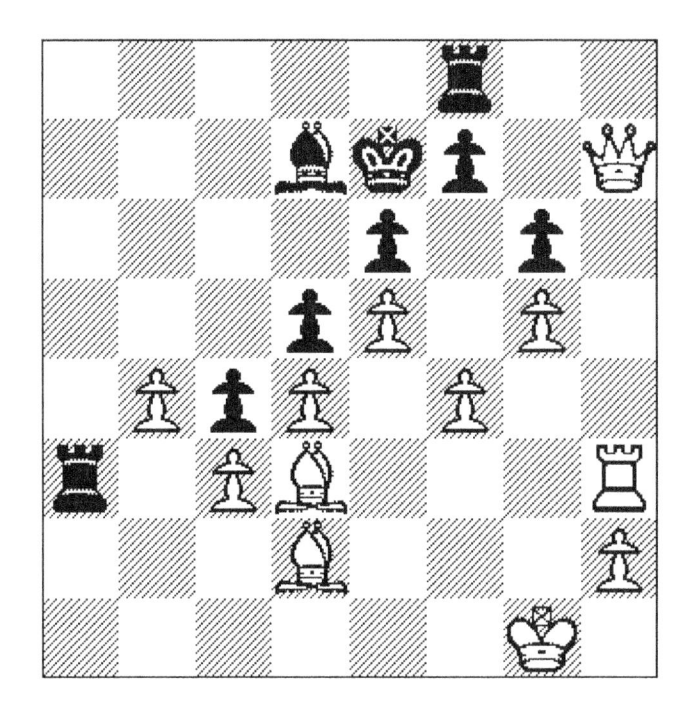

After 48...cd3 49. Kf2, followed by Qg7, black is hopeless.

Game 28
Astounding chain

February 9th 2015
White: Lyudmil Tsvetkov
Black: Stockfish 6
A07 Reti Opening, King's Indian Attack

**1. Nf3 Nf6 2. g3 d5 3. Bg2 e6
4. O-O Be7 5. d3**

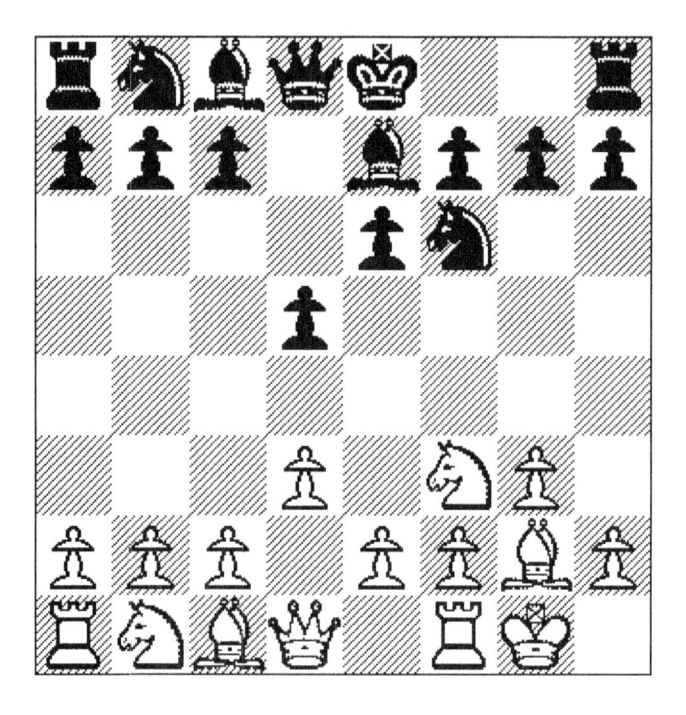

5. d4 is weaker.
White gets its favourite King's Indian setup.

O-O 6. Nc3 c5 7. e4 Nc6

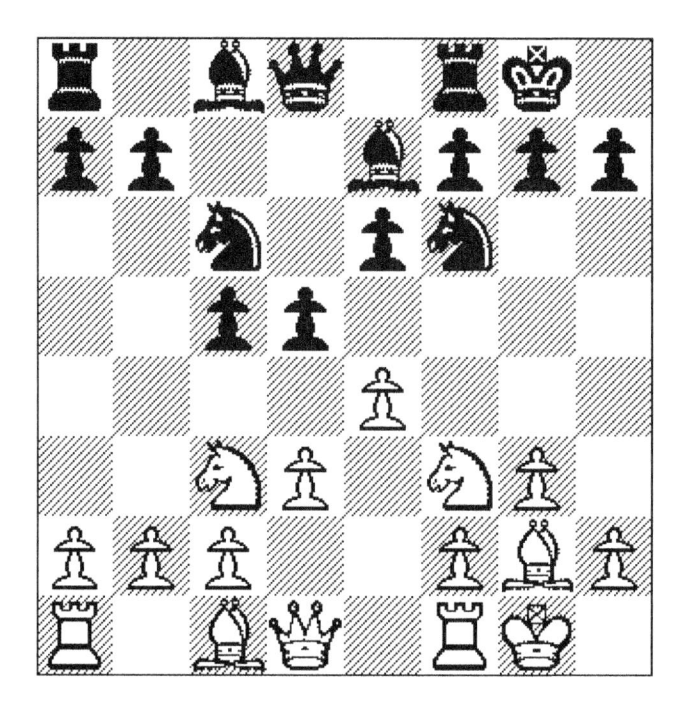

White might have gotten a Fischer-like structure after 8. e5 Nd7 9. Re1, but it hopes for more.

8. Bd2 d4

As said, de4 is the only realistic chance to equalise.

9. Ne2 e5 10. h3

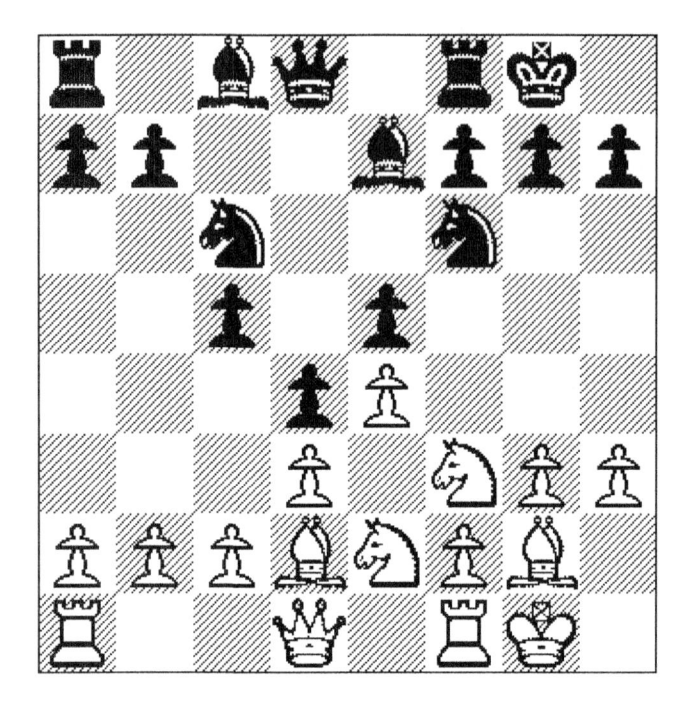

The bishop is not welcome to g4.

Nd7

10...c4 was an interesting try. White will have to play Ne1 and f4.

11. Ne1

Still doable.

b6

Stockfish develops.

11...f5 12. ef5 Rf5 13. g4 Rf8 14. Ng3, and white takes possession of the e4 strong point.

12. f4

White is already significantly better.

Passive as it might seem, the bishop on g2 has taken long-range aim at the knight on c6 and rook on a8, for possible tactics, in case the long diagonal gets opened.

Ba6

To counter with c4.

13. b3

Preventing that.

f6 14. f5

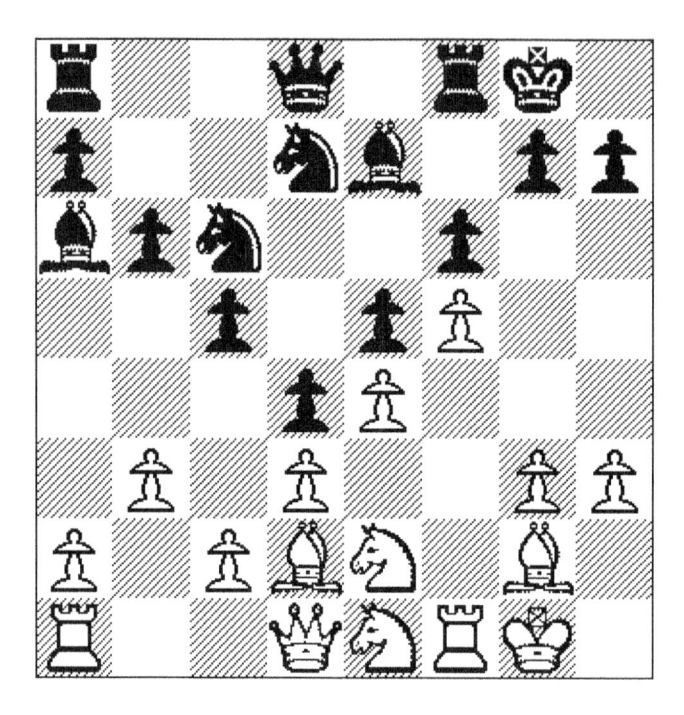

The longer pointed chain has been built.
From now on, white will only increase the pressure.

**Bb7 15. g4 a6
16. h4 Rb8 17. Nf3**

The bundle of white pieces starts unravelling.

b5 18. Ng3 c4

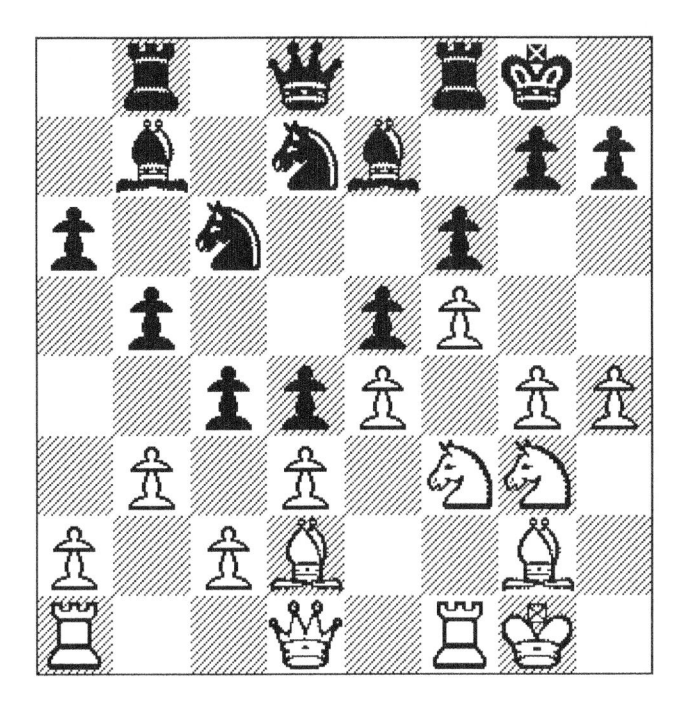

Although seemingly not exhibiting multiple threats, the position is very complicated.

19. Kh1

Clearing the g file.

c3

This seems like a mistake, as Stockfish closes the queen side, where it will lack counterplay.

19...cd3 20. cd3 has been called for, though it is unclear how black continues to pressure after that.

20. Bc1

Be1 was an alternative. Ba3 g5.

Nc5 21. a3!

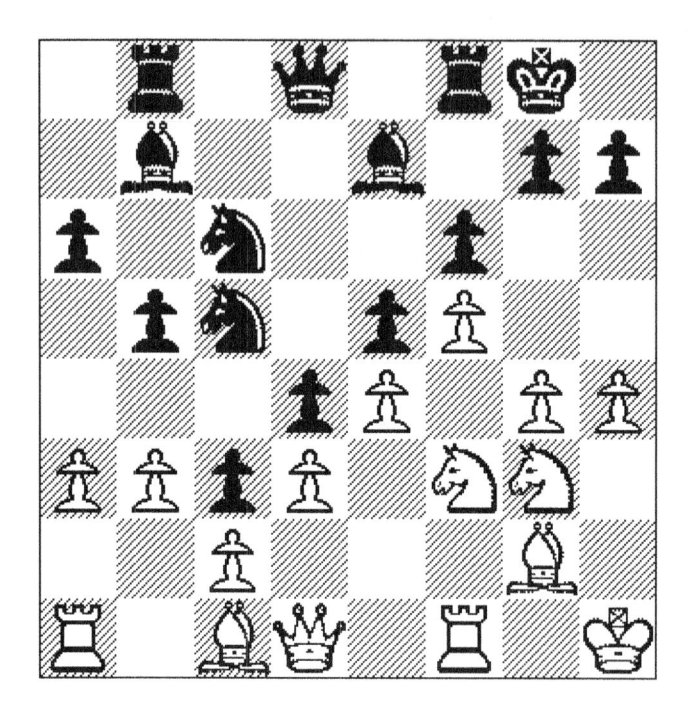

So that, after a6-a5, a5-a4 is met by b3-b4, while b5-b4 by a3-a4, fully closing that section of the board.

One white disadvantage is that the a1 rook is artificially trapped, because the bishop on c1 has nowhere to go.

For the time being.

h6

g4-g5 has been threatening.

White's space advantage on the king side is much more important than black's space advantage on the queen side, as the kings are there.

22. Bh3

Clearing the g file and getting the bishop to a more active place.

In similar closed positions it is very important to be able to regroup one's pieces effectively.

Nd7 23. Qe2 Kh8

In order to play Rg8.

24. Nh5

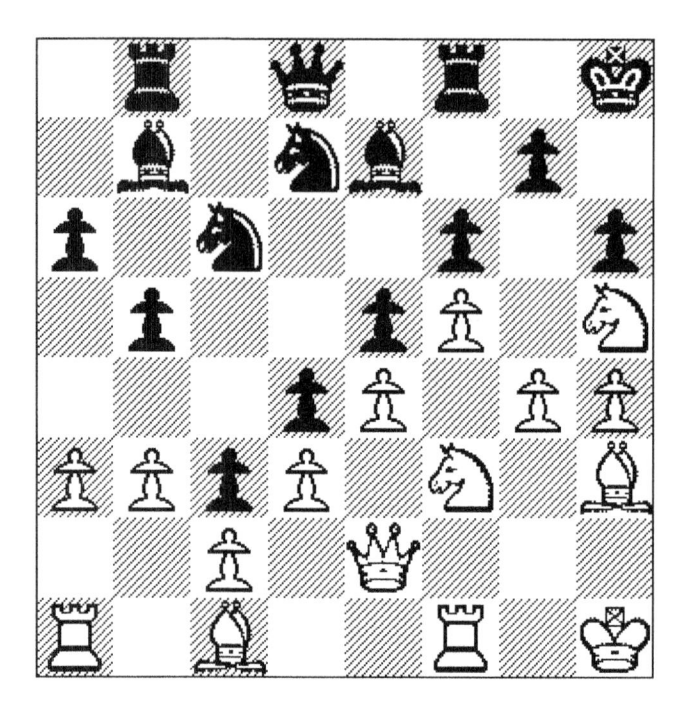

The knight takes aim at g7.

Qe8

Attacking the knight, so g4-g5 becomes impossible.

25. Rg1 Qf7 26. Ng3

Taking a step back, to make two forward.

Bd6 27. Rg2

To attack via the h file.

Rg8

Black has no option, as too many squares are weak, g6, h6, etc.

28. g5

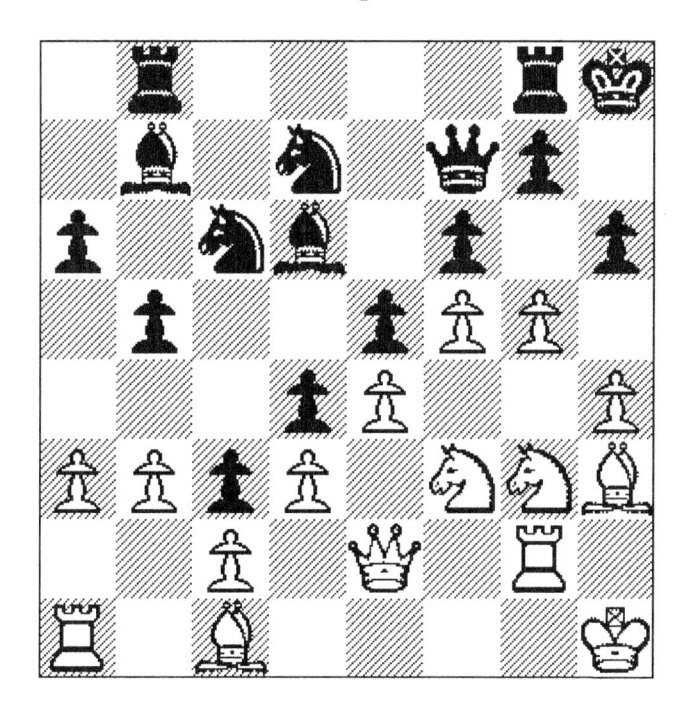

Black is completely helpless.

Bf8

The bishop defends the h6 square.
On 28...g6, both 29. fg6 Rg6 30. h5, followed by g6, and even 29. h5 win.

29. g6!

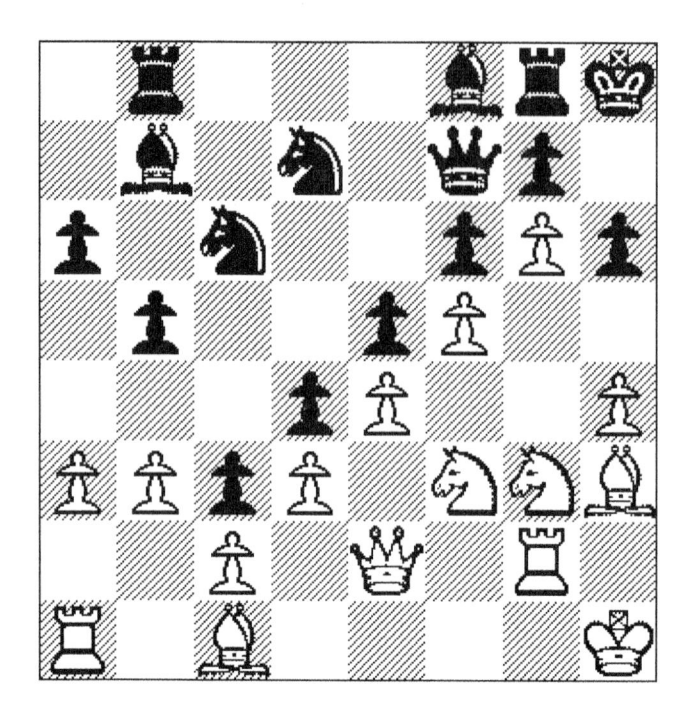

The c2-d3-e4-f5-g6 longer chain is astounding.

The black g7-f6-e5-d4-c3 long chain is astounding too, but fully dysfunctional.

Qe7 30. Nh2

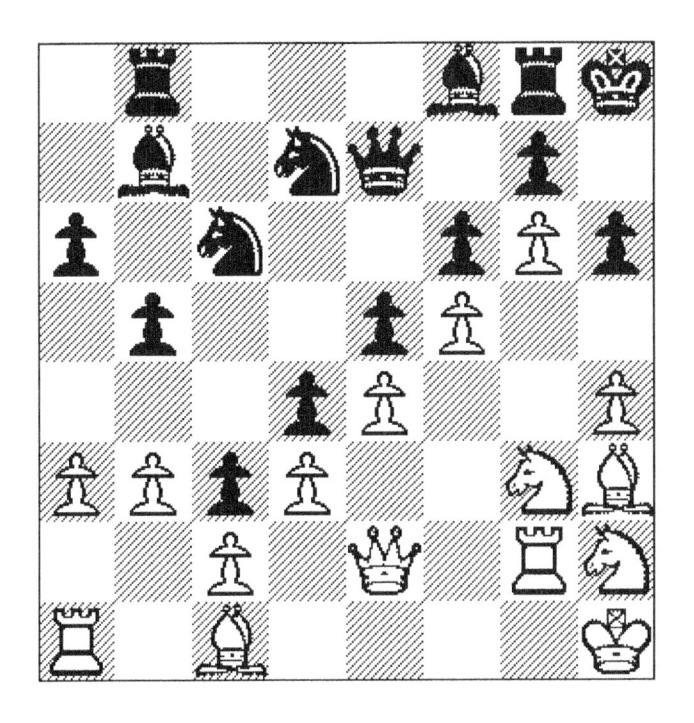

Final dislocation.

The queen heads to h5, while the knight to g4, to deliver the decisive blow on h6.

b4

There is simply no escape.

31. a4

Qh5 straight was also winning, but that only underscores black's helplessness.

Rd8 32. Qh5 Bc8 33. Ng4

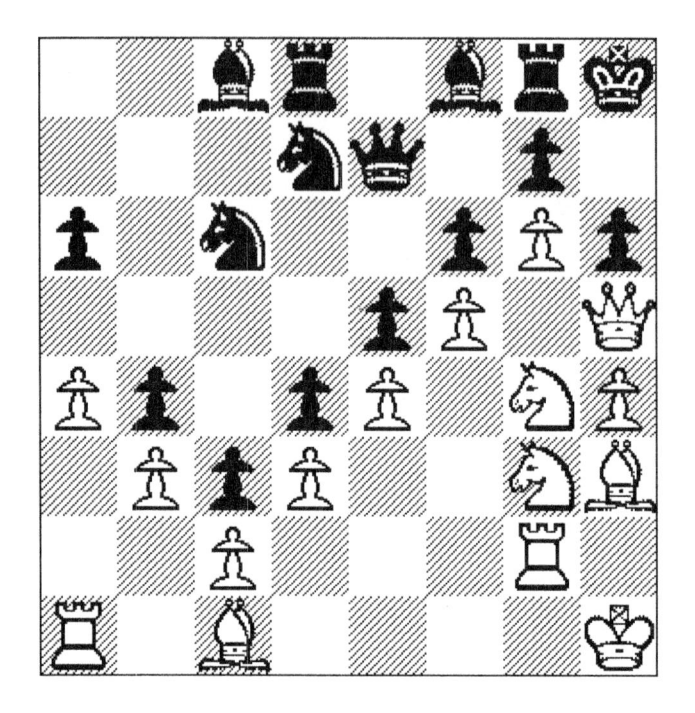

Astoundingly, not a single piece or pawn has left the board yet.

Nc5 34. Nh6

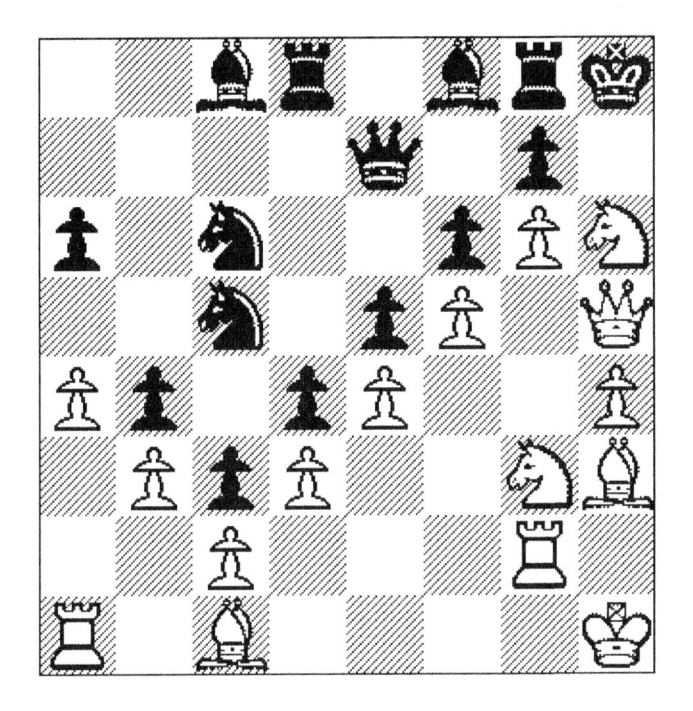

No comment.

gh6 35. Bh6

Stockfish resigned.

Mate in 2 or 3 is unavoidable(the longest line being Qh7 gh7).
36. Bf8 threatens.
35...Rg7 36. Bg7 and Qh7 mate.
35...Bg7 36. Bc1

Game 29
Positional squeeze

August 8th 2016
White: Lyudmil Tsvetkov
Black: Komodo 10.1
A46 Queen's Pawn Game, Torre Attack

1. d4 Nf6 2. Nf3 e6 3. Bg5

The Torre Attack is a strong one.

c5

I would prefer Be7, followed by h6.

3...h6 4. Bf6 Qf6(gf6 is inadequate) 5. e4 will more or less lead to developments as in the game.

4. c3 Nc6 5. e3

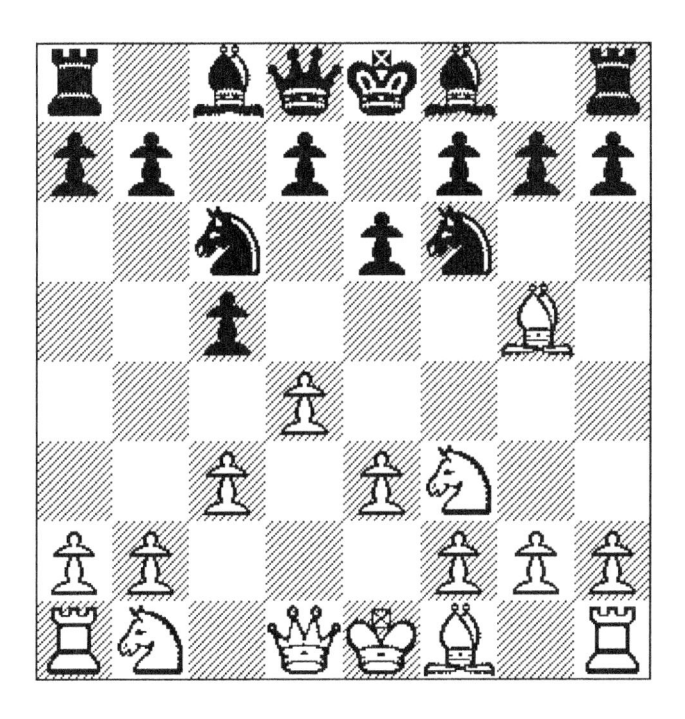

Now, on cd4, white can capture ed4, opening the e file for the rook.

h6 6. Bf6

Of course, Bh4 g5 is weaker.

Qf6

The place of the queen is simply not on f6.

7. Bd3 d5 8. O-O Bd7

Black develops.

9. Nbd2

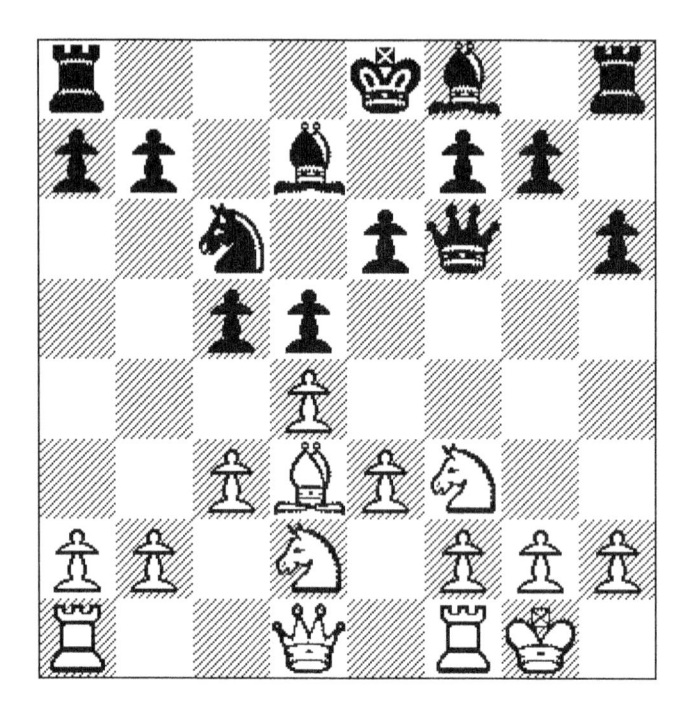

Let's take stock of this position.

White has a stronger center(twice defended d4 pawn), plus a lead in development. Besides, the black queen is awkwardly placed. That more than compensates for the pair of bishops.

cd4

That is obviously an inaccuracy, as opens the e file for the white rook.

9...Be7 10. dc5 Bc5 11. e4 de4(otherwise white isolates black's central d5 pawn with ed5 ed5, which is a major disadvantage) 12. Ne4 Qe7 13. Nc5 Qc5, followed by Qe7 and castling short, ensures white just a small edge.

9...e5 is premature, as after 10. de5 Ne5 11. Ne5 Qe5 12. e4, black struggles to complete development.

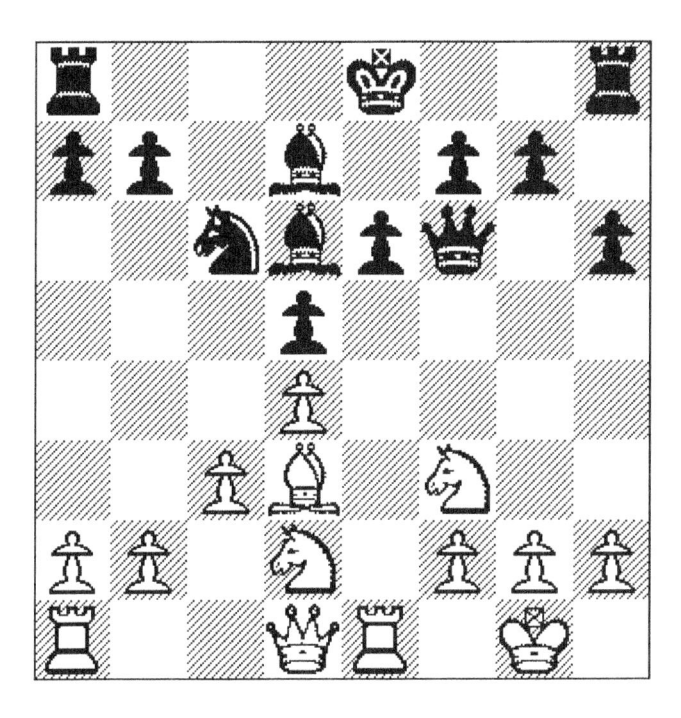

10. ed4 Bd6 11. Re1

Indeed, the rook takes aim at the e5 square.

O-O 12. Qe2

209

Controlling e5 once again, so that e6-e5 break is currently impossible.

White threatens to install a knight on e5.

Qd8

Tacit admission that Qf6 has been awkward.
Now, the queen at least guards the bishop on d7.

13. Ne5

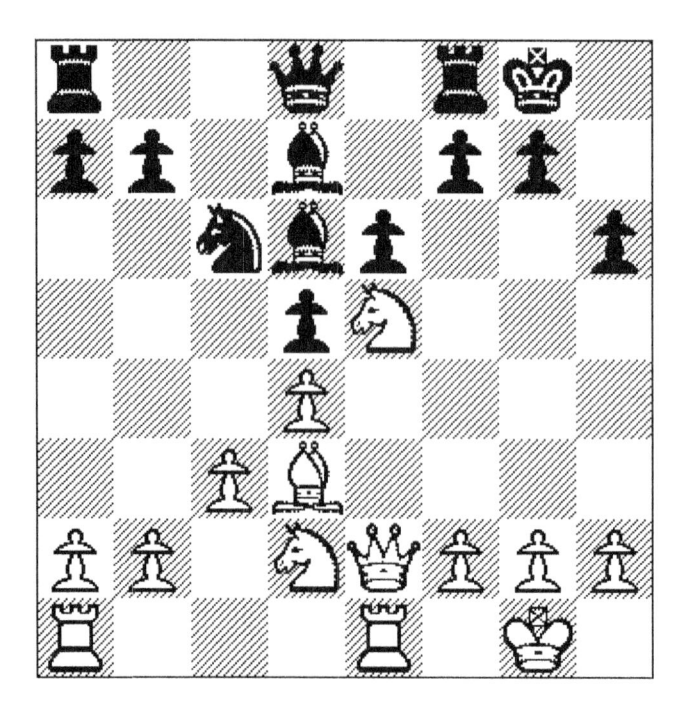

A power-jump on e5.
White's advantage is clear.

It is difficult to put up with such a knight for a longer time, and f2-f4 threatens.

The knight also can not be driven away with f7-f6 at any point, as this leaves behind too many weaknesses.

Ne5

Seemingly, nothing better.

14. de5 Bc7 15. Nf3

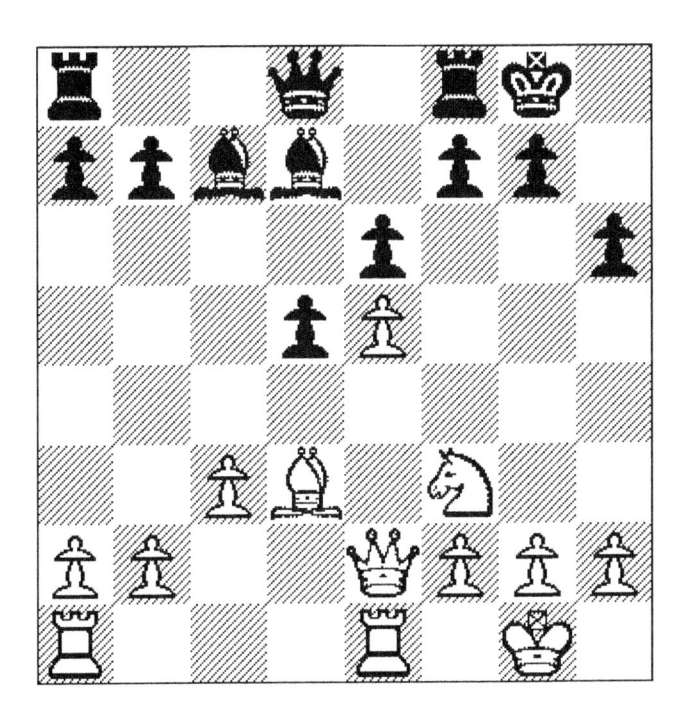

Heading to d4.
f4 is premature.

Rc8

16. Rad1

Centralisation.

Ba4

Attacking the rook on d1.
Maybe, white will trade its much stronger light-square bishop with Bc2, or weaken its pawn structure with b3.

17. Rd2

Nothing of the sort.
The rook feels fine on d2.

a6 18. Bb1!

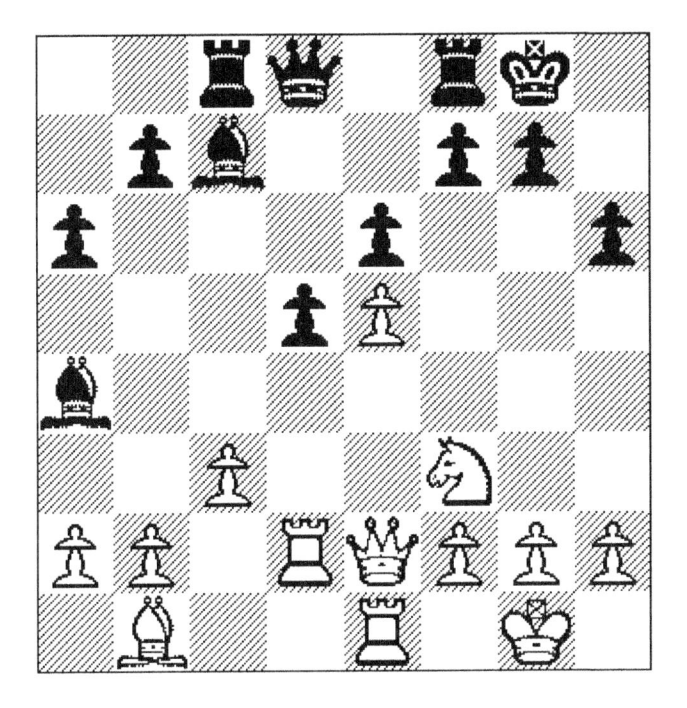

Qd3, further weakening black's pawn structure with g6, is prepared.

Bb5

The queen will not go to d3.

19. Qd1

Maybe to c2, then?

g6

Forestalling Qc2.
No other defensive option is available.

This, however, significantly weakens the f6 square.

20. h4!

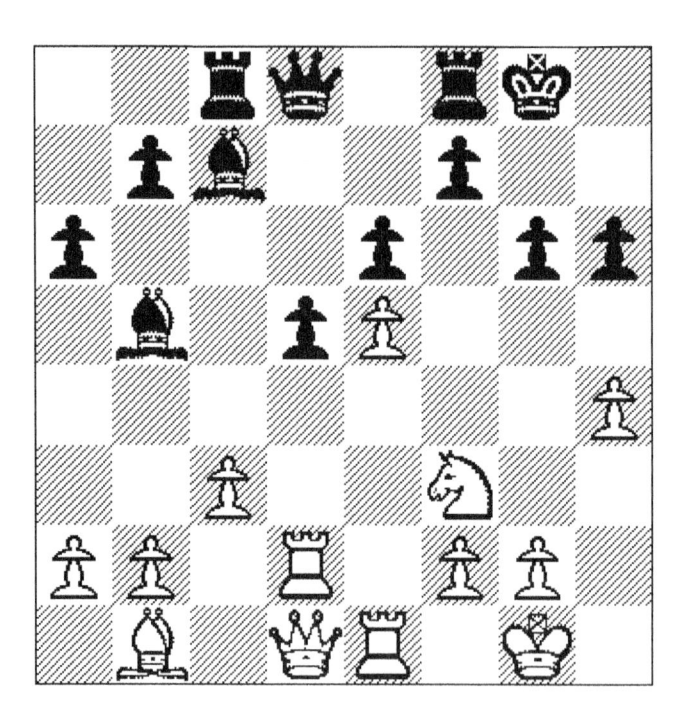

The sooner, the better.
h4-h5 threatens.

h5

No other option.

21. Rd4

The rook lifts, not to the 3rd, but to the 4th rank. The f4 square is targeted.

Bb6

Expelling the rook.

22. Rf4

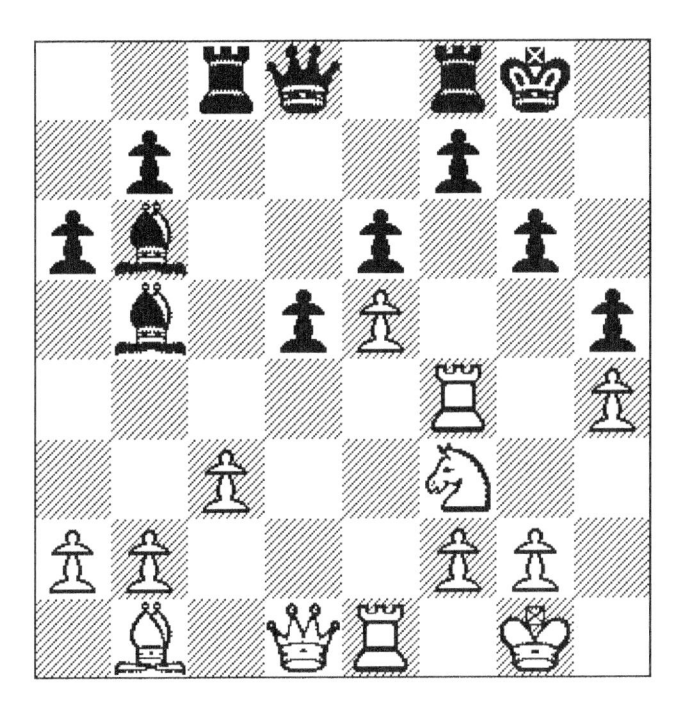

The black position is riddled with weaknesses. The rook threatens to penetrate on f6.

Bc5

To guard the f6 square after Bc5-e7.

22...Rc4(challenging the white rook) was an alternative, but after 23. Rf6 Rg4 24. Qd2 Kg7(otherwise, the queen penetrates on h6) 25. Ng5, white has multiple threats, for example Rg6 fg6 Ne6, picking up the queen.

23. Qd2

h6/g5 are x-rayed.

Be7 24. g3

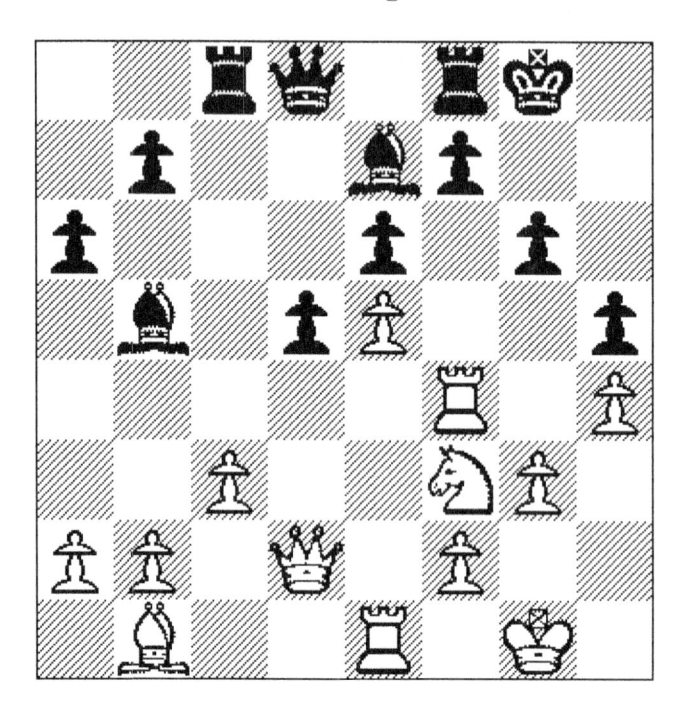

Prophylaxis.
Supporting the h4 pawn.
There is no hurry, black lacks any counterplay.

Bc6

Rc4 Nd4, and then Re3-f3.

25. Nd4

The plan is good now too.

Bd7 26. Re3 Qb6

At least to attack the b2 pawn.

27. Ref3

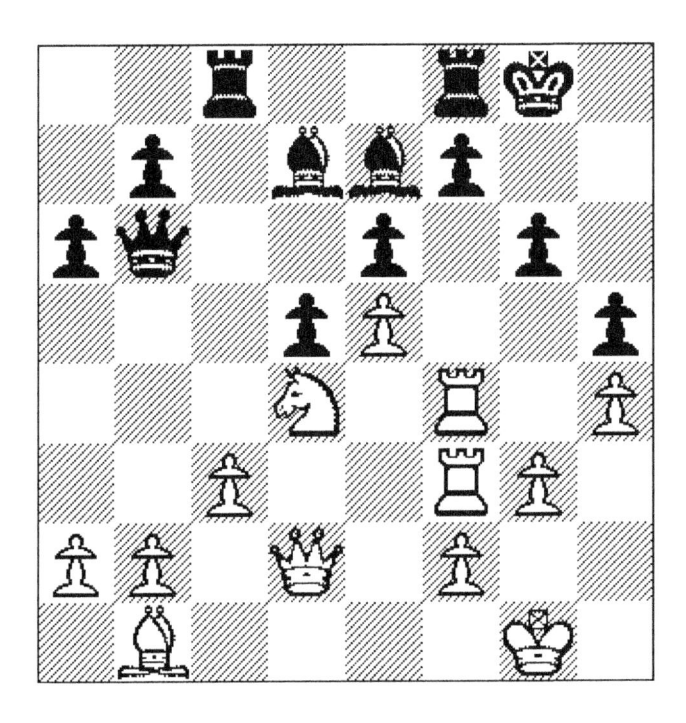

The white position is so powerful, it is difficult to imagine black can last more than a dozen moves.

Qc7

Attacking e5.

28. Qe3

e5 is protected.

Qc5

Komodo obviously sees nothing, but there is no defence one way or another.

29. Rf6

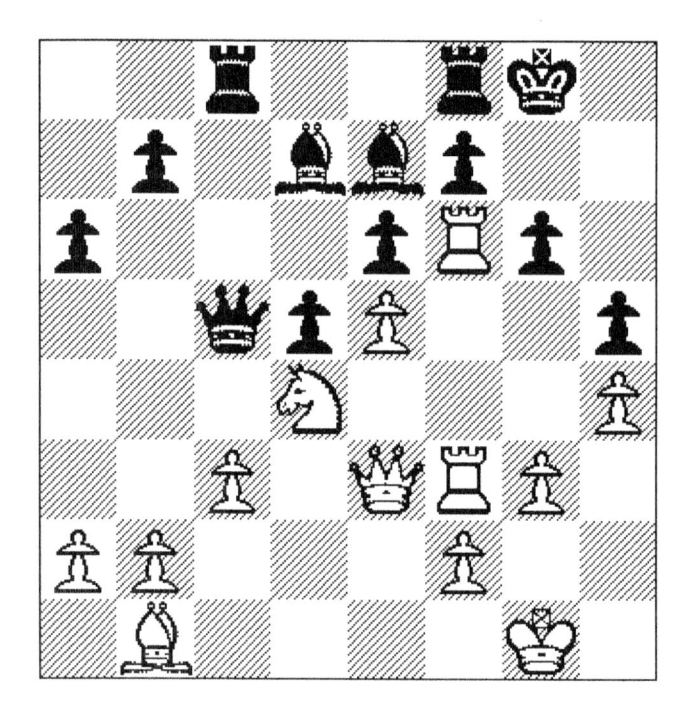

Black is busted.
Qh6/g5 are lethal.

Bf6

29...Be8(to defend the g6 pawn) loses quickly to 30. Qh6 Qc7 31. R3f5!(that works too) ef5(gf5 Qg5 check and Rh6 mate) 32. Nf3 and Ng5.

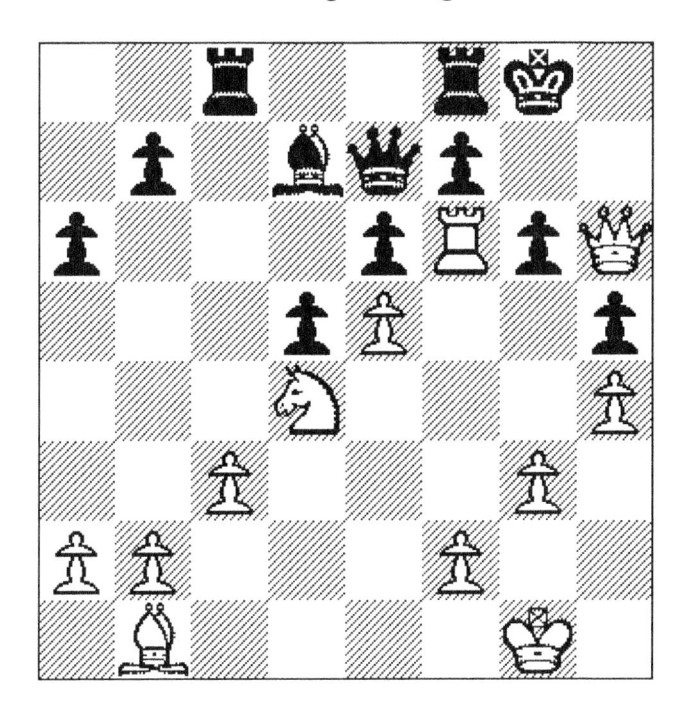

30. Rf6 Qe7 31. Qh6

Bg6 threatens.
You think Komodo is so powerful?

Rc4

32. Bg6 fg6 33. Rg6

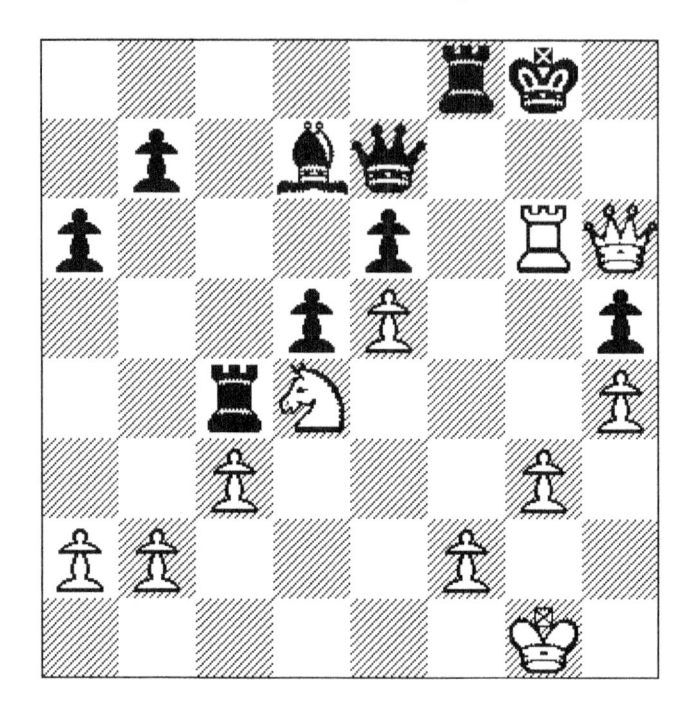

Black resigned.

33...Kf7 34. Qh5 leaves black defenseless(Re6 threatens).

Game 30
Hitting the ball with the bat

August 12th 2016
White: Komodo 10.1
Black: Lyudmil Tsvetkov
B31 Sicilian, Nimzovich-Rossolimo Attack

**1. e4 c5 2. Nf3 Nc6
3. Bb5 g6 4. O-O Bg7 5. Nc3**

This is a weak move, that blocks the c pawn and abandons any central claims.

c2-c3 was much superior.

e5!

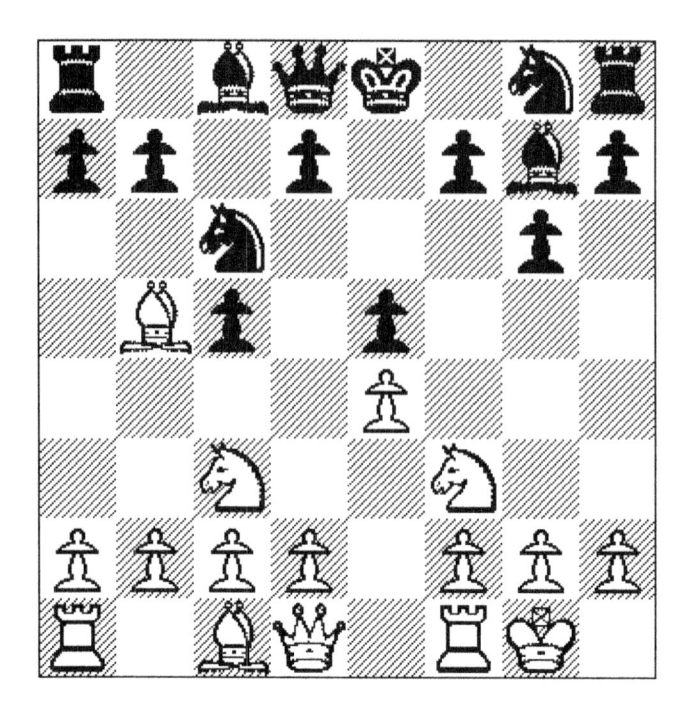

Of course.
d4 is strongly bound, black is already better.

6. d3

There is no other choice.
White should develop slowly.

Nge7

Preparing to castle.

7. a3

Freeing the a2 square for the bishop after a possible a6 Bc4 b5, but also targeting b4, for a potential b2-b4 wing pawn storm.

Black should take measures.

a5!

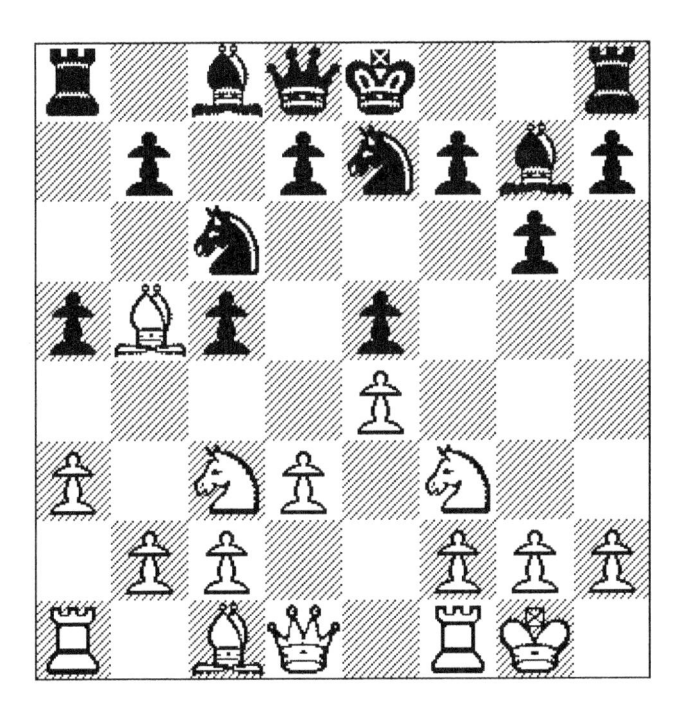

No b4 is allowed.
That would weaken black's grip upon the d4 square.

8. Bc4

Targeting f7.

O-O 9. Nb5

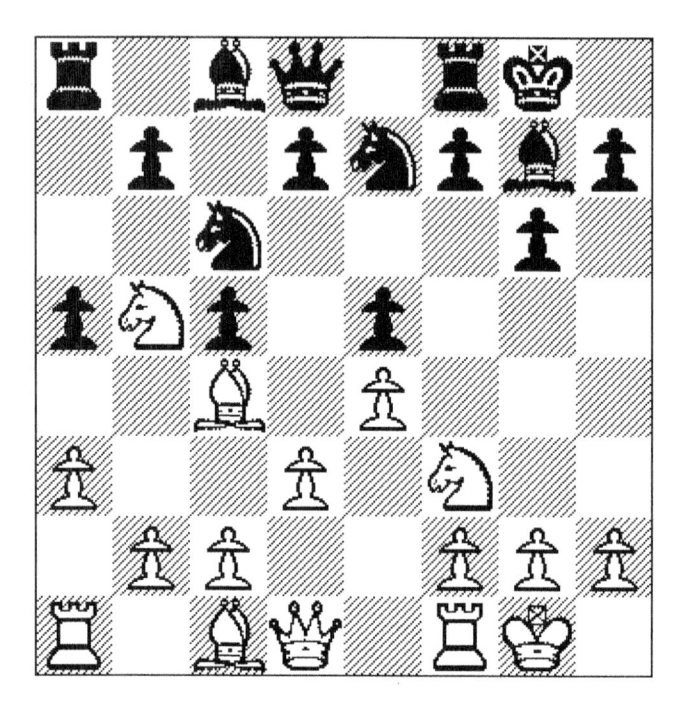

That looks strange.

Obviously, Komodo overvalues some outposts.

9. Nd5 d6, followed by h6, Kh8 and f5, is not much better, though.

d6

Of course, black will not allow the knight to land on d6.

10. a4 h6

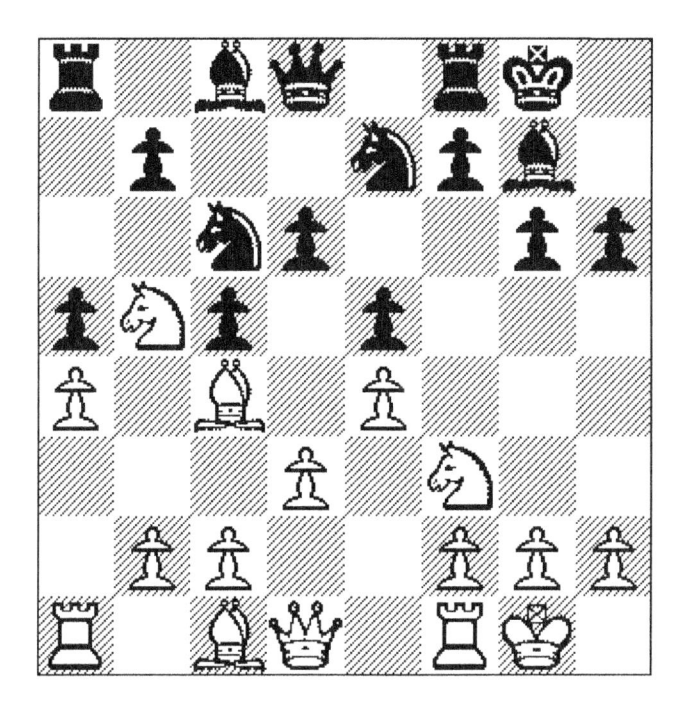

The g5 spot is forbidden ground for both the bishop on c1 and the knight on f3.

11. c3

d3-d4 should be attempted, otherwise white has no counterplay at all.

Kh7

Might be even stronger than 11...Kh8, as after a possible Nh4 jump, the knight targets the g6 square with check in some lines.

12. Be3

Too slow.

Black retains a superior position after 12. d4 cd4 13. cd4 Bg4, but that is precisely how white should have continued.

f5

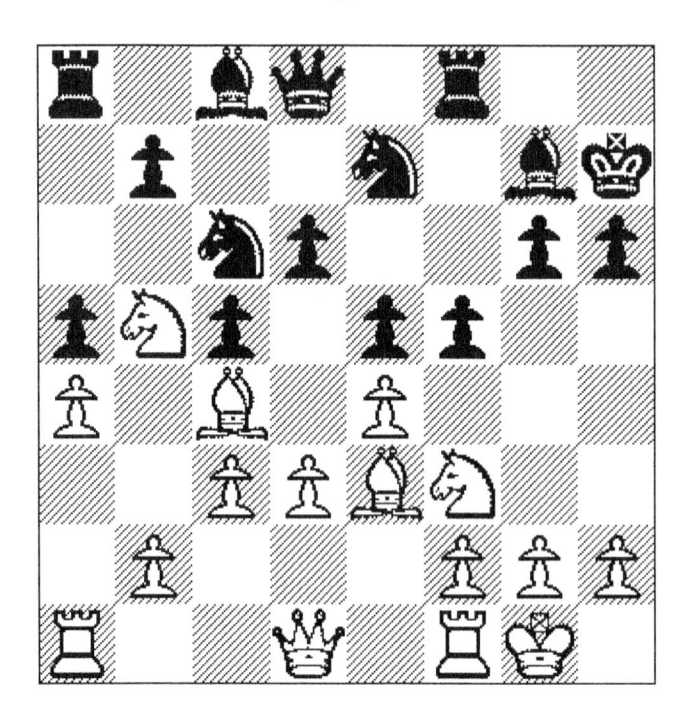

[chess diagram]

Black's advantage has increased to large.

d3-d4 is impossible now, because of fe4, and black threatens f4.

13. Bd2

The bishop has to retreat.

f4 14. h3 g5

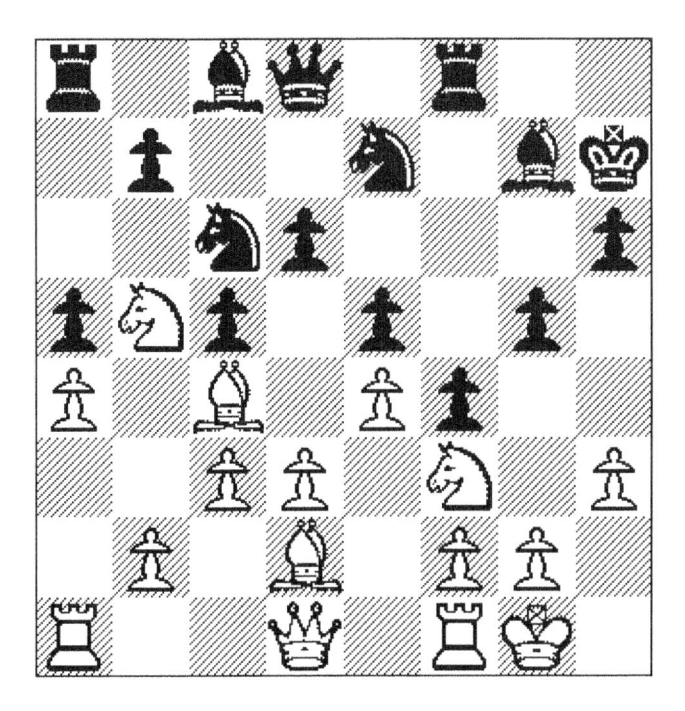

Although the its king is fairly unprotected, black has thrashing advantage.

g5-g4 is extremely unpleasant.

15. Qb3

Komodo decides to attack along the free long diagonal.

15. Ng5 hg5 16. Qh5 Bh6 does not work.

15. Nh2(to stop g4 and h5) was a realistic alternative, though black retains big edge in all lines.

One continuation is Ng8-f6(capturing the knight on g8 with the bishop does not make white's life any easier), followed by h5 and g4.

Sacrificial attempts, involving Qe8-g6 manoeuvre, and then h5 and g4, are also possible, but black should be very careful in similar variations.

Alternatively, black can play Qd7, Rd8(to defend the d6 pawn), and only then Qe8-g6(Rb8 might be included first, to avoid the fork on c7).

Ng6

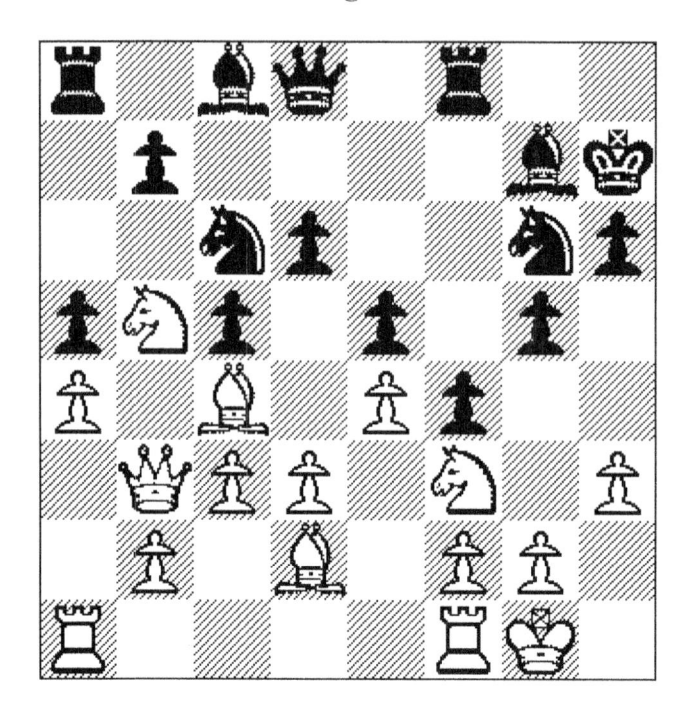

Not so much to get the knight to a more active position, rather than to support the g5 pawn with the queen, so that h5 becomes possible.

16. Bf7

Komodo is in an attacking vein.

Qe7

Avoiding any unnecessary complications that could arise after 16...h5 17. Nd6
Who knows how this could end, especially in a faster game?
Komodo is invited to take the g6 knight.

17. Bd5

The engine is reluctant to do so.
Bg6 Kg6 trades much weaker knight for a stronger bishop, and the black king will soon return to safety.

h5

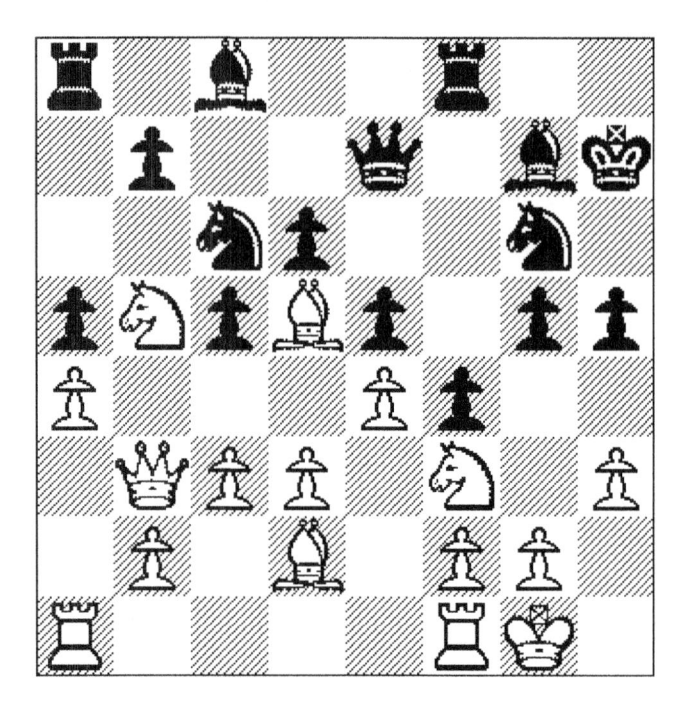

Black is on a roll.

18. Nh2 g4

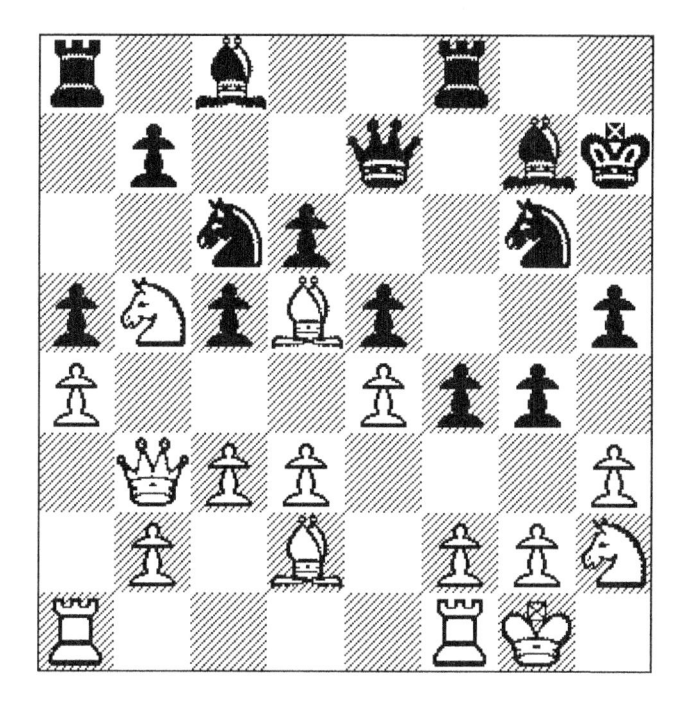

Not a chance in the world to save that.

19. hg4 hg4

The h file gets opened.
The black heavy pieces will soon penetrate there.

20. g3

Black threatens Rh8, f3, Qh4, etc.
20. f3 g3 is hilarious.

f3

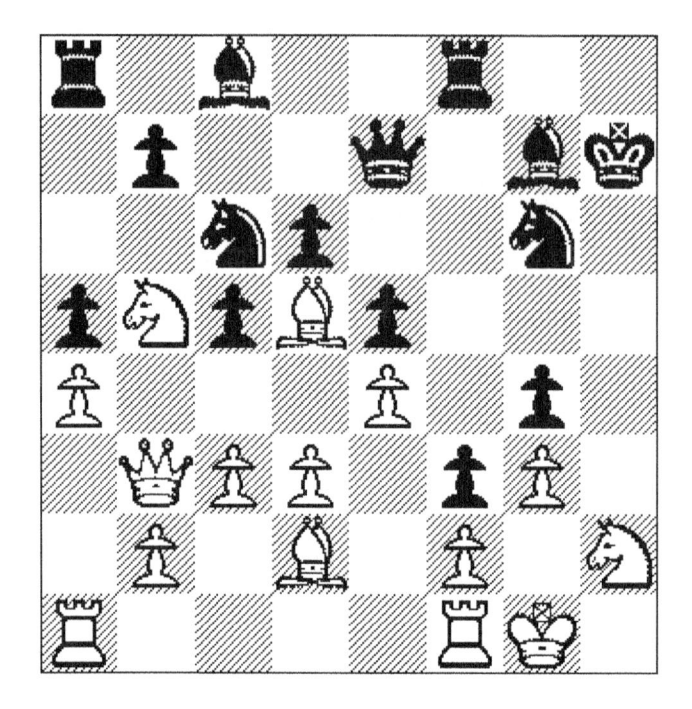

The white king is caged and its fate is spelled.

21. Na3

After a possible Nc4-e3, the knight will guard the g2 square.

Bh6!

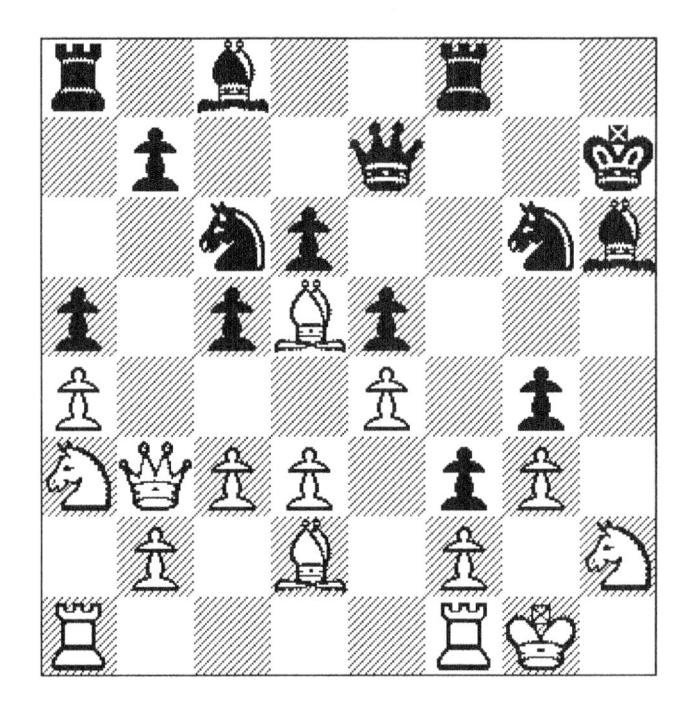

Clearing the g7 square for the king, so black can play Rh8.

22. Be3

Capturing the bishop does not help in the least.

Kg7

White can only dream of Be3 fe3, followed by Rf2, defending the knight on h2.

23. Bh6 Kh6 24. d4

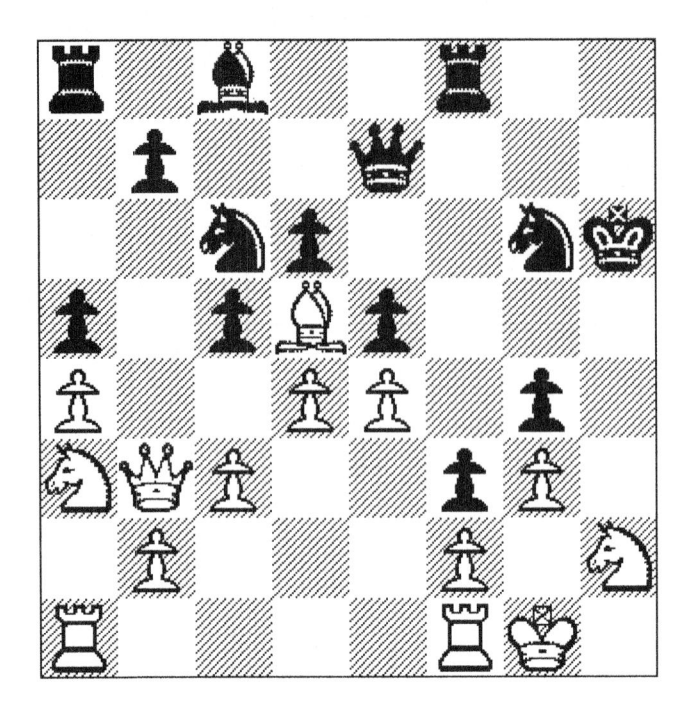

A very belated central thrust.

Whoever does not challenge the center early on, will never do so.

Kg7 25. dc5 Rh8

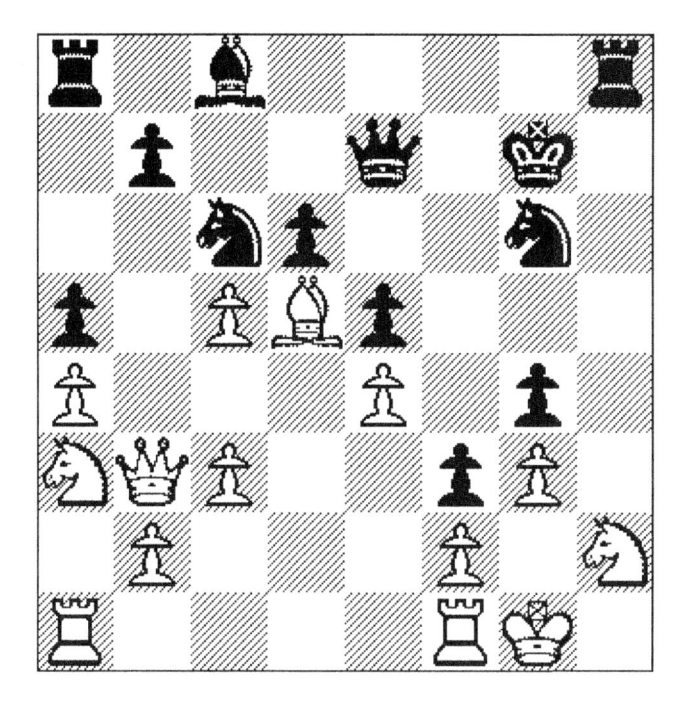

Qg5-h5 is unavoidable.

26. Nb5

Heroes die in a shuffling mode.

Qg5 27. Bg8

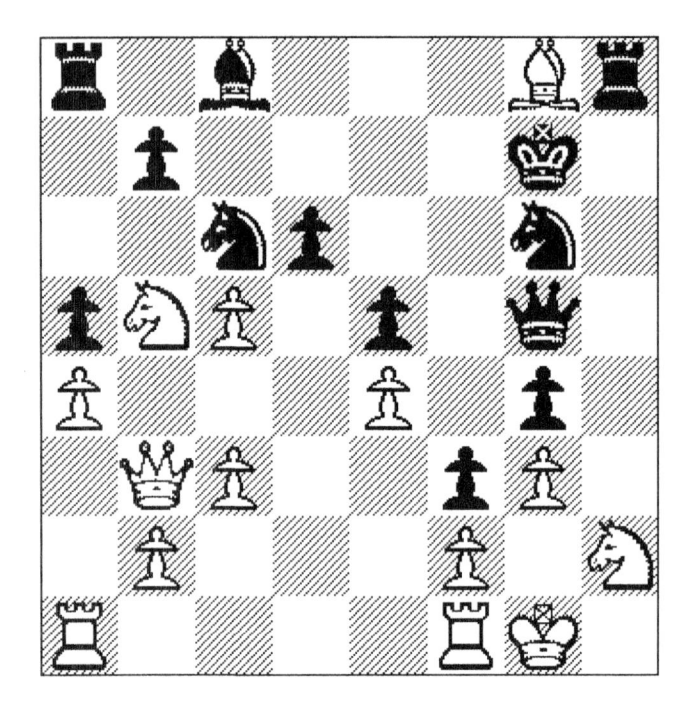

Tricky, white threatens Qf7 check.

Nd8!

The knight controls the f7 square to prevent the check.

It is not necessary to invite more checks after Rg8 Nd6, or research complications ensuing after Qh5 Qf7.

28. Bh7

Komodo is resourceful.

Rh7 29. Rfd1

29. Nd6, followed by Ne8/f5, might gain white couple more spite checks.

Rh2

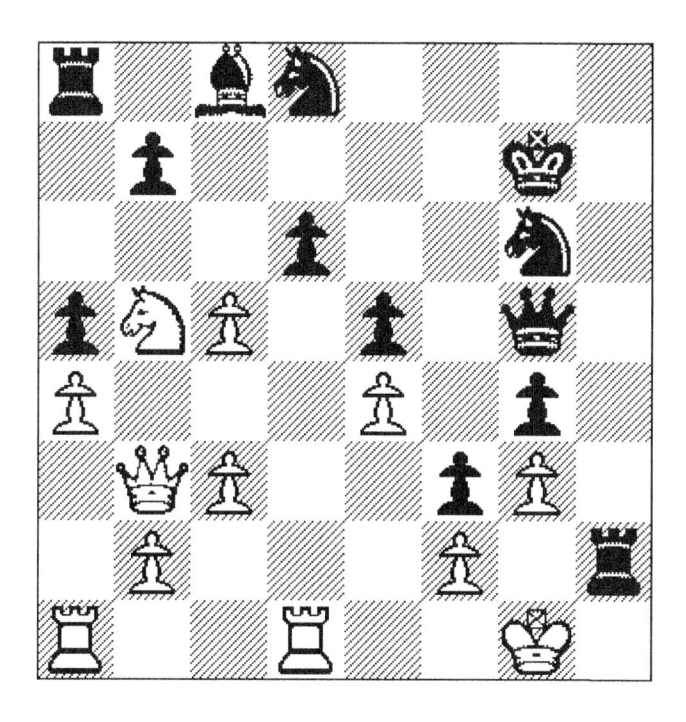

Komodo resigned.

Kh2 Qh5 Kg1 Qh3 mates on g2.

Index of Games

Game 16: Lyudmil Tsvetkov - Stockfish DD
Game 17: Lyudmil Tsvetkov - Stockfish DD
Game 18: Lyudmil Tsvetkov - Stockfish DD
Game 19: Lyudmil Tsvetkov - Stockfish DD
Game 20: Lyudmil Tsvetkov - Stockfish DD
Game 21: Stockfish DD - Lyudmil Tsvetkov
Game 22: Lyudmil Tsvetkov - Stockfish DD
Game 23: Lyudmil Tsvetkov - Stockfish DD
Game 24: Lyudmil Tsvetkov - Stockfish 5
Game 25: Lyudmil Tsvetkov - Stockfish 5
Game 26: Lyudmil Tsvetkov - Stockfish 5
Game 27: Lyudmil Tsvetkov - Stockfish 6
Game 28: Lyudmil Tsvetkov - Stockfish 6
Game 29: Lyudmil Tsvetkov - Komodo 10.1
Game 30: Komodo 10.1 - Lyudmil Tsvetkov

Printed in Great Britain
by Amazon